VINCENT TAYLOR

Sassafras Neck
A Special Place in Time

VINCENT TAYLOR

Printed by CreateSpace

Copyright © 2017 Vincent Taylor

All rights reserved.

Manufactured in the United States of America

ISBN-13: 978-1977743763
ISBN-10: 1977743765

NOTE: The information in this book is true and complete to the best of the author's knowledge. It is offered without guarantee on the part of the author or his heirs and/or family members. The author, his heirs/family and the publisher disclaim all liability in connection with the use of this book.

All rights reserved. No part of this book may be reproduced or transmitted in any form whatsoever without prior written permission from the author's designees (family members) except in the case of brief quotations in critical articles or reviews.

Cover photo (mouth of Scotchman's Creek at Bohemia River)
Courtesy of Mike Dixon, Historian

CONTENTS

	Acknowledgments, Foreword, Preface	i-xiii
Chapter I	Geography of Sassafras Neck	15
Chapter II	Resources of the Neck Area	19
Chapter III	People of Sassafras Neck	23
Chapter IV	Occupations in Sassafras Neck	27
Chapter V	Farming and Agriculture	31
Chapter VI	Hunting, Fishing and Trapping	43
Chapter VII	The Tradesmen	53
Chapter VIII	Hog Killing Time	61
Chapter IX	The Country Store	67
Chapter X	Home and Family Life in the Neck	79
Chapter XI	Education in Sassafras Neck	89
Chapter XII	Country Doctors and the Cecilton Drug Store	101
Chapter XIII	Religion and Johntown Church	107
Chapter XIV	Recreation of the Sassafras People	119
Chapter XV	The Economic Depression	127
Chapter XVI	War Efforts in World Wars I and II	135

Chapter XVII	The End of Old Time Farming and Lifestyle	143
Chapter XVIII	Realtors, Developers and Radical Change	149
Chapter XIX	Marinas and Boat Action	155
Chapter XX	Bygone and Present Times	161
	About the Author	167
	Historic and Noteworthy Locations	169

ACKNOWLEDGMENTS

A heartfelt thank you goes out to all of the people who helped make this book possible: for her editorial and publishing assistance, book coach Michele Chynoweth; for their help in supplying photos and other historical or technical information the following organizations and individuals—The Historical Society of Cecil County, The Maryland Historical Society, The Cecil County Public Library, The Cecil Whig Newspaper, The Friends of the Turkey Point Lighthouse, Barratts Chapel Methodist Museum, The Cecil College Library, The Chesapeake Bay Maritime Museum, David Bliss Photography and Photo Restoration, Carol Donache, Michael Schoenbeck, Josh D. Brooks, Michele Reed Cole, Jenifer Dolde, Amy Henderson, and Kraig Anderson; and last but not least to Ron Taylor who pulled it all together and brought it to fruition.

VINCENT TAYLOR

FOREWORD

Our father wrote this book you hold in your hands in the mid-to late-1980s before he passed away at the age of ninety-one.

It was important to him that we, his children, make sure it was published not only to leave us a legacy, but to share with the world how precious life was in the 19th and 20th centuries in the area known as Sassafras Neck in Maryland's Chesapeake Bay area—how life was simpler then, when folks worked on farms and waterways.

We hope whether you are young or old that his memoir recaptures this special place in time to educate you in its history and culture, and that it will encourage you to better appreciate good old-fashioned work ethics, the value of nature—both of the land and sea—and the importance of church, education, family and community, so that these things can perhaps be preserved, recreated, and not lost forever.

—With love, his children, Vincent L. Taylor, Ronald L. Taylor and Susan (Taylor) Reed

VINCENT TAYLOR

PREFACE

I was born and raised in the Sassafras Neck area of Cecil County Maryland, as described in this book. As a young boy, and over the years, I have tramped, explored and worked on farms, fields, woods, waters and marshes of Sassafras Neck. I have worked on farms in corn and wheat fields, hay and pasture fields, plowing, cultivating and harvesting many different crops, and I hunted, trapped, fished and crabbed in both the Bohemia and Sassafras rivers. This land and shores between these two rivers is Sassafras Neck, as we knew it.

I always knew this area was a beautiful, special little piece of land between the two rivers. I decided to document this area and its people as they were in my times. My family encouraged me to follow through, so on many winter nights I documented the life and times of these by gone days.

Sassafras Neck and its people have changed quite a bit in my eighty some years. Not all of that change has been good. The old "Neck" and its people and times are gone for good. Farming is now a much bigger operation with its bigger equipment. Farms have been sold off in tough times to developers for housing developments, while old farmhouses, barns, and out buildings have been torn down for bigger fields and more tillable acreage.

The face of Sassafras Neck and its people have changed forever more, so my hope in writing this book is to recapture this long gone place and time so that it won't be forgotten.

—Vincent W. Taylor (1912 - 2003)

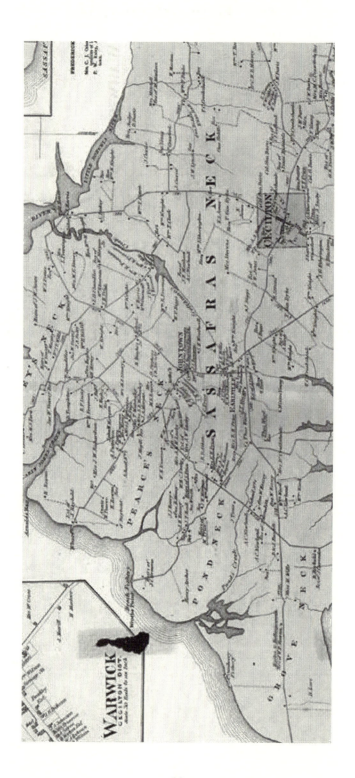

CHAPTER I
GEOGRAPHY OF SASSAFRAS NECK

Looking at a map of Cecil County in the state of Maryland, one will notice an area of land in the very south end of Cecil County, at the head of the Chesapeake Bay between the Bohemia and Sassafras Rivers, which for many years has been referred to as Sassafras Neck. This neck of land is just about the start of the real Eastern Shore of Maryland. With its creeks, low lands, and marshes, the west outer end faces the head of the bay and has been generally referred to as the upper end of the Eastern Shore of Maryland. This neck heads up east and is bound by the Delaware state line.

Sassafras Neck, especially on the westerly portion, is made up of other smaller necks such as Grove Neck, between the Sassafras River and Pond Creek; Pond Neck, between Pond Creek and Pearce Creek; Pearce Neck, between Pearce Creek and Cabin John Creek; and Veazey's Neck, between Cabin John Creek and the Bohemia River. The general starting point for going into these necks is a village called Earleville, with the exception of Veazey's Neck, which mostly starts at the south end of the Bohemia River bridge or what used to be Bohemia Wharf. Coming up the Sassafras River, looking to the southerly side of Sassafras Neck, one will see Money's Creek, Foreman's Creek, Back Creek, and several other smaller creeks or guts up to Fredericktown that head up into marshland. Pond Creek, Pearce Creek, and Cabin John Creek were larger creeks heading in from the head of the bay and the mouth of the Elk River. For the most part, these writings will be more or less concerned with the four smaller necks mentioned above, referred to as the west end of Sassafras Neck starting at the village of Earleville.

Many years ago, before the coming of the white man, this well-watered area of land with its creeks, woods, and marshes teeming with fish and game was inhabited by Indians. This was evidenced by the findings of thousands of arrowheads, stone axes, and other stone artifacts which, over the years, have been pretty well picked up. These Indians were, in old times, known as the Tockwaughs.

As happened everywhere else in the United States, the coming of the white man, with which most Indians could not cope, caused the Indians to leave the area, except for a small band which our elders talked about. They were somehow bypassed or isolated on a small peninsula halfway between the Sassafras River and Fredericktown, with the river on one side and Back Creek on the other side, called Knights Island. In those days, quite a few native Indians could easily subsist on game and fish, wild fowl, roots, bark, berries, and many other wild growing things.

As time went by, this small band of Indians and the early white settlers became somewhat intermingled, and as a result, a few of us now native whites living in the west end of Sassafras Neck have a few drops of Indian blood in our veins. According to my elders, my great-grandmother on my father's side was pretty much all Indian except for his white man's name, which is my name, Taylor.

The Taylors were a family in Sassafras Neck going way back. I will say that I am not ashamed of my little bit of Indian blood and neither were my elders. Otherwise, most of the old-time settlers in the neck were mostly English with some Irish and Scotch Irish mixed in. There was probably a sprinkling of Swede spilling over from what is now nearby Delaware as well as a little bit of German from Pennsylvania.

In the early days of white settlement in Sassafras Neck,

considerable amounts of the land, as in other areas of Maryland, were given as grants from England, no doubt to various English gentry. Later, as families developed, most of the land was owned and controlled by prominent families. Eventually, marriages between members of prominent families and members of less prominent families caused the land to be divided into smaller tracts of land referred to as farms.

These farms were, on average, two to four hundred acres in size, with some having more or less acreage. The farms of this size held up until the middle of the 1950s. We will see, later on in this writing, what took place with the farms.

As time went on, cities like Baltimore, MD, Wilmington, DE, and Philadelphia, PA were growing. Many of the descendants of the old prominent families left the neck to be educated, and as a result many of them stayed to live in the cities. Eventually, much of the farmland was inherited by the families of those who had moved to the cities. It seemed that a lot of the land was owned by strangers, and indeed a lot of these people were strangers to the land. Back in those days, the west end of Sassafras Neck was considered "boon docks" by the city folk.

To close this first chapter, a little should be mentioned about Maryland's northern boundary line. Between the years of 1763-1767, two land surveyors, Charles Mason and Jeremiah Dixon, ran the line that fixed the northern boundary of Maryland to the southern boundary of Pennsylvania, and this line was recorded in history as the Mason Dixon line. It was also set down as a line that divided the thirteen colonies into the north and the south. Maryland has always been looked upon as a southern state, however even as of recent times, many Maryland people in the northern and western part of the state don't seem to realize that they live in a southern state.

In present times, the Mason Dixon line would be thought of as the dividing line between the northern states and the southern states of the east coast. Mason and Dixon also did the survey work for the boundary line between eastern Maryland and Delaware. Even today, just a few of the old boundary markers are still standing as the line runs adjacent to the east end of the Sassafras Neck area. So from the foregoing, one can get an idea of the geography of the Sassafras Neck area and also of the early settlers.

Mason Dixon Line Marker

CHAPTER II
RESOURCES OF THE NECK AREA

In the west end or outer area (toward the bay) of Sassafras Neck, the resources were fairly bountiful as were the assets of the headwaters of the Chesapeake Bay—the creeks, marshes and wetlands. These resources and assets included farmland, woods and timber, wild life, and fish and game. To look at these resources in order, we will start with the farmland.

Even though the west end of the neck was not a large land area, the soil varied somewhat. Farmland deep in the smaller necks had somewhat sandy and loamy soil. A little further up neck where land was a little roily, the soil was mixed with gravel areas from which several gravel pits were opened and the material used to put in farmhouse lanes, country dirt roads, driveways, etc. A lot of the soil was just plain good dark top soil with occasional small boulders. Some of the soil was on the poor side, being referred to as white ground, and still another type had a lot of stones and clay in it. The two latter types were farmed and tilled, but were not a favorite with the farmers. However, the land fertility was not considered too bad.

The west end of Sassafras Neck, as mentioned earlier, was bounded by the head of the bay. This was a very valuable asset for the reason that, in the early spring of the year, shad and herring came up the bay to spawn in the fresh and unsalted waters at the head of the bay and in the Elk, Bohemia, and Sassafras Rivers. The pound-net fishermen trapped these fish and they were sold at the fish markets and directly to the neck people. Catfish, yellow and white perch, pike, bass, sunfish, and eels were plentiful in the creeks and rivers. Crabs were abundant in the early years up into the 1940s, and rockfish and carp were also plentiful.

The bay side and rivers were also valuable because there were many areas where channels ran deep and fairly close to the shore lines, so piers and wharves could be constructed to accommodate steamers, schooners, and other bay and river craft which greatly aided transportation.

The marshes and wetlands also greatly contributed to the area's resources, as they were the home of the muskrat, which in the early days were very plentiful. The muskrat was trapped for fur, which could be sold for a good price and was also used for meat. The marshes were also the home for the snapping turtle. The snapping turtles grew to weigh as much as forty pounds, some even weighing fifty pounds. The snapping turtle was edible and was sold as a delicacy in many fashionable restaurants. The red-belly snapper, which weighed about two to four pounds, when fried like chicken was also a very appetizing dish.

The marshes harbored many wild ducks, rail birds, and reed birds. The bald eagle, the osprey, or fish hawk, and numerous other types of hawks frequented the west end area, not as a resource, but by nature—maintaining a need for ecological balance in the marsh, creek, river, and bay areas.

The woodlands were another very good resource. The woods contained stands of timber, and it worked out that just about every farm in the west end area had a piece of woods on it. The larger the farm, the larger the woods. These woodlands had a great variety of wood, such as the oaks, beeches, hickories, gums, ashes, wild cherry, cedar, pines and other types of trees. These woods furnished timber for barns, stables, houses, and other buildings, bridges, wharves, boats, and also provided fuel for heating purposes.

Many farms had an area at the head of the woods, usually with a stream of water where only a few scrubby trees grew, and low ground where a good cover of grass grew, known as meadows. These meadows were greatly valued by the farmers for grazing cattle and raising tame geese and ducks. Many of these meadows abounded with blackberry bushes, which most every farm family picked and canned for winter use.

Most of these resources were respected and not abused in earlier days and were still fairly abundant into the 1920s and 1930s. Then with World War II, happenings in the west end of Sassafras Neck caused many changes which saddened the local people and depreciated, overcrowded, and to some degree, polluted the whole west end of Sassafras Neck and its creeks, rivers, and the head of the bay.

At the head of the bay, looking at a map, one will see that four rivers run into the head of the bay—the Sassafras, Elk, Northeast, and Susquehanna. The peninsula that runs down between the Elk and Northeast Rivers has always been called Elk Neck and it ends in a cliff point stabbing into the head of the bay, which is called Turkey Point.

On this point, over many years, stood a tall lighthouse known to mariners and watermen as Turkey Point Light, and it was a very important light as it seemed to say at night when lighted, "I stand here to warn that this is the head of the bay—watch where you go." Many west end natives always liked to look across the water to see its bright light at night. Built in 1833, the light house still stands. However the farm house nearby was torn down and the original light beacon was replaced with a more modern type of navigational light. The old light was, for most of my lifetime, attended by a woman named Mrs. Salter, who is now deceased. She was well known and friendly to many of the neck people.

Sassafras Neck was a fine area for "country" living—for farming, fishing and hunting in woodlands, meadows, marshland, rivers and creeks—and for many other things applicable to a country style of living. One of God's especially bountiful and beautiful areas, it was but one of many across the country. I have always felt good about being born and raised in this area on the upper Eastern Shore of Maryland referred to as Sassafras Neck.

Turkey Point Lighthouse

CHAPTER III
PEOPLE OF SASSAFRAS NECK

In the first chapter, somewhat of the genealogy of the neck people in the earlier times was mentioned. This chapter will concern the people of later times, from the 1860s to the 1960s, which goes back to my grandparents and to my own later life. From the late 1800s to the early 1900s, the largest class of people were the farm folk, mostly of English and Irish stock and a few Scotch, many or most of whom had descended from the early settlers of Sassafras Neck.

Native names included Davis, Bailey, Taylor, Craig, Haggerty, Wooleyhan, O'Neal, Matthews, Pearce, Husfelt, Manlove, Williams, Oldham, Price, Frazer, Dixon, along with many other English, Irish, and Scotch names.

During the late 1800s, a few people migrated to the Sassafras Neck area from Kent County across the Sassafras River. My own grandfather came from Queen Anne's County when he was nineteen years of age, along with his father, mother, brothers, and sisters and the family's few black servants, to rent and till a farm at the Veazey's

Cove area in Veazey's Neck on the Bohemia River.

Most of the farm village people were in some way related to one another by kin or by marriage if one looked back a generation or two or three. Just about all of the farmers and tradesmen types of people in the west end of Sassafras Neck were by religion mostly Methodist; that is to say the ones that adhered to church going.

Another type or class of people in Sassafras Neck were more or less of the old gentry type, who seemed to be, or at least claimed to be, descended from the early English gentry, such as the Veaseys, Foremans, and Calverts under Lord Baltimore. Most of this type of people owned, by inheritance, many of the Sassafras Neck farms, which they rented out to what was referred to as tenant farmers, which will be mentioned later in this writing, and were Episcopalian by religion. Catholic folks were in a very small minority in the west end of Sassafras Neck.

A lot of black people were also already here by reason of a more or less mild form of slavery to serve the early gentry folks. However, the Negroes that we will mention most in this writing are from 1860 to the early 1980s. Many or most were descendants of freed slaves. Many of these black people came to Sassafras Neck as migrant workers from the state of Virginia and were referred to as Virginia Negroes. Some of them liked it here and many stayed here permanently and raised families, and from them descended our black citizens of today with last names such as Gatewood, Cisco, Hall, Bacon, Coates, Wise, Boyer, and Brinkley.

The religion of the black folks was a Methodist type which consisted of camp meetings a few times a year, but in the early 1900s they acquired a church building in Cecilton and the old style camp meetings ceased to be held, except for very special occasions.

Then as was mentioned in Chapter I, a few of us neck people had forefathers who had married into the Indian population that was living in the Knights Island area, of which this writer derived a few drops of Indian blood. As a whole, the neck folks—both black and white—got along well with one another and never had any racial trouble between them.

We must also mention the fishermen that were part of the neck population. They were the people that fished in the bay, rivers, and creeks for a living, with various types of nets, such as fike nets, gill nets, and haul seines. Some of these men were loners and lived in shanties down along the creek and river shores.

Since people had diseases and illnesses come upon them from time to time; I will mention a few of those hardships. If one goes through the older sections of the local cemeteries, looking at the tombstones and the inscriptions on them, one would notice that many people died at a young age. Much of this was probably due to the lack of physicians and insufficient knowledge at that time of the dangerous diseases and illnesses even into the 1900s. Many young people just above and below twenty years of age died of consumption (tuberculosis), pneumonia, diphtheria, typhoid, fever and influenza, and many children died of whooping cough.

Today, of course, most of the above diseases can be cured if they are not neglected too long. It must be said though, that many a life was saved by housewife wisdom and the use of herbs, juices, teas, wines, and whiskeys. Also, back in the early times and up until approximately 1925, very little cancer and heart trouble was known.

All in all, all of the people on the neck were like one great big family. As mentioned before, most of the people from Earleville on down the neck were in some way related to each other just like one big family made up of a lot of smaller families. So, due to this family type of lifestyle, when a member got ill the family took care of them. Hospitals were almost nonexistent and nursing homes were unheard of. For example, my grandparents on my mother's side took care of both of my great-grandmothers at the same time when they were very old and unable to do for themselves, and this was common among the Sassafras Neck people.

Susie and Vince Taylor

CHAPTER IV
OCCUPATIONS IN SASSAFRAS NECK

The people of the Sassafras Neck area were engaged in several types of occupations. The greatest number of people were involved in farming the land, and in later years many farmers had dairy cattle herds. Some farmers owned their land while others were tenant farmers renting the farms, in most cases, from farm owners who had inherited the land but did not do any farming themselves and lived mostly in the larger towns and cities of Wilmington, Delaware and Baltimore, Chestertown and Elkton, Maryland.

Some of the old gentry descendants owned as many as four, five or six farms and acted as overseers of their farms and tenants. The sons of farmers usually followed in their parents' footsteps and also became farmers into the 1920s more or less, except a few who went into the cities to do other work.

Almost every farm had a large farmhouse to house the farmer and his family. Most farms had another smaller house and sometimes two, in which a hired farm hand and his family lived; these were referred to as tenant houses. Some of the large farms required a lot of help. These hired tenants were, in most cases, black people—usually a man and wife and several children. Many times, the white children and black children played together and you might say grew up together and lived in harmony. There did not seem to be any racial troubles.

There were several people engaged in carpentry work building barns, stables, cow sheds and other smaller buildings, and new houses here and there in Earleville and Cecilton. These carpenters worked alone, in pairs, and for the large buildings and houses, by families of brothers which had learned and inherited the trade from their fathers and brothers.

Carpenters, in the late 1800s and early 1900s, were very fine workmen who took much pride in their work. They did their own plastering, masonry, and foundation work and could also lay a good brick chimney. Working in that fashion in contemporary times would probably be considered a cardinal sin among the unionized tradesmen of today. Many men who were not farming were painters working on houses, barns, stables and other farm buildings, and even churches.

Some of the farmers had their own sawmills set up in their woods. Then sometimes a logging and sawmill outfit from outside the neck would be allowed to set up a mill and cut some timber. This work, in times previous to about the 1930s, was carefully done, and after the trees were felled and logged, the leftover wood or smaller tree limbs were split into chunks for firewood. The remaining brush was piled up, under which many rabbit and bob-white quail found shelter in bad winter weather.

In my lifetime, a large blacksmith and wheelwright shop was located in Earleville. During my early life this business was operated by my father and his brother and, previous to them, my grandfather owned and operated the business. At another site (Grind Stone Corner) and way before my time, my great grandfather established and operated the original Taylor blacksmith shop. Another smaller blacksmith was also in business in Earleville during the 1920s and 1930s. Up neck, in the town of Cecilton, there were two blacksmith shops, one of which was operated for many years by my father's uncle.

These shops shod many horses, mended iron work, built wagon bodies and harrows, repaired wagons, buggies and Dearborn's, made and repaired wheels, and even repaired children's wagons and metal toys. In the late 1920s, due to the advent of the automobile, farm tractor, and mechanization in general, blacksmithing and wheelwrighting soon went out of existence.

A few people were engaged in the gristmill industry. There was one business in particular that served the west end of the neck, and was located about two and one-half miles north of Earleville. The proprietor was known to everyone as "Dusty." He was a big, robust, and jovial man and was also known to have a big appetite, but everyone liked Dusty. Here is where (in my earlier days) everyone took wheat to be ground into flour and corn to be ground into cornmeal. This type of business also died out as modern times rolled in.

The country store was a flourishing business from the early times in the 1800s into the 1930s. A large general store was located in Earleville, which for the most part served the west end of Sassafras Neck. Another smaller store was located at Watts Corner down in Pond Neck. Up neck at Cecilton, at one time during my earlier life, there were four general stores, a farm machinery and hardware store, a harness shop, and one grocery store located in the Negro section.

Another grocery store/post office combination was located in Fredericktown. A post office was located in the general store in Earleville, which served most of the west end people. Another post office was located in Cecilton, and yet another in the town of Warwick, also in a grocery store. There were two other general stores and one hardware store in Warwick, which is near the Delaware state line.

A few people were engaged in fishing and trapping commercially. Sometimes the farmers, when they weren't trapping, rented out their marshland (if they had any) to trappers who did pretty well trapping muskrats, raccoons, and foxes in the wintertime and then fishing in the creeks and rivers with their various types of nets, traps, and haul seines in late winter and spring. They sold their catches locally to fish peddlers and to the fish markets. Another type of fishing was done in the rivers and at the head of the bay by using large pound nets. Some of these fishermen came up from Tilghman's Island every spring and hired many of the local men to fish with them as it took a sizeable crew to set and fish with one of these big nets that hung on large poles stuck into the river bottom.

There was plenty of occupational activity going on in Sassafras Neck. When I was a boy, unemployment in Sassafras Neck was just unheard of. The neck's topography of farmland, creeks, marshes, rivers, and the bay invited all kinds of employment. There were jobs in farming, marine work, lumber, fishing, carpentry, country stores and many other fields, all country type jobs that tied in with the basics of life there; there was not a tall belching smoke stack or factory anywhere in the confines of Sassafras Neck.

Just about all the occupations in the Sassafras Neck area meshed into one other, with farming being the backbone.

J.R. Taylor Blacksmith Shop & Store Earleville, MD

CHAPTER V
FARMING AND AGRICULTURE

This chapter will be concerned with the occupation and business of agricultural farming in the area of the Sassafras Neck peninsula which includes the farming of milk cow herds and in the later years, the switch (with some farmers) to beef cattle herds.

The Sassafras Neck farms were mostly two hundred to four hundred acres in size. Most of the farms, however, had about the same number of farm buildings which ranged in size, and most of the farmhouses were plain "L" shaped two-story clapboard houses with ample attic space. Some of the real old farmhouses that were constructed in the late 1700s to the middle 1850s were the old brick masonry type houses, built for the old gentry type of people and their families. Some of these old mansion style houses still stand today, with most having been restored. The barn, or granary building, was usually large with upper and lower levels.. Most were constructed with large double doors at each end of the building so that two-horse farm wagons could drive inside to unload corn into the two large cribs on either side on the first floor and to unload wheat, oats, barley, or rye by block and fall rig, to be hoisted up through a large open area in the left floor to be put into large separate areas called bins.

The next large building was the horse stable, also a two-story or two-level facility. Arranged on either side were stalls for separating the horses. Each stall had a manger bin for hay and a feed bin for a ration of corn or other grain. Some stables would house four horses on each side, or larger stables could house six on each side.. In between these stall areas there was a much more narrow area where the workmen could walk up and down to put feed into the mangers and grain boxes. The upper level of these stables was one big open space, where hay was stored for winter feed. The end of the stable opened to the barnyard, the other end into the farmyard.

The stable served as a fence along one side of the barnyard, and on the other side was the cow stable, a one-story building. This, also was arranged inside so that eight to twenty cows could be positioned side by side for feeding and milking.

On yet a third side of the barnyard there was usually a plain open shed that opened into the barnyard with wood rails laid loosely on top on which sheaves of fodder were stacked to serve as a winter roof. So, three sides of the barnyard were completely fenced in by buildings keeping out most of the cold winter winds and making shelter for the animals in winter. The yard was bedded down with straw, also for winter warmth.

The smaller buildings were usually hog pens built in a hog lot or in the corner of an orchard used to pen up the hogs in the fall of the year for fattening in preparation for butchering. In the farm yard, there would be a rather long open faced shed for storing the farm machinery and various equipment out of the weather. This building had only a dirt floor. There was also a poultry house or two, as every farm in those days had a flock of poultry and laying hens.

Near the farmhouse, there was always a small building called the meat house where all the hog meat was stored to dry and cure. Many farms also had an ice house. This was a square hole dug into the ground about eight to ten feet deep, lined along the sides with wood planks, a roof built over top and the pit itself filled with straw. Chunks of winter ice cut from rivers and creeks were hauled up in wagons and put under the straw. The ice would keep all summer and was used in making iced tea, lemonade, and homemade ice-cream. The carriage house, or (in later years) the garage, was usually a closed section on one end of the farm equipment shed.

Last, but not least by any means, was the family outdoor toilet or privacy house, which, of course, in recent modern times was abandoned when plumbing, heating, and bathrooms were installed in the farmhouses.

Many farms had two wells for water—one at the vicinity of the back porch of the farmhouse with a wooden hand pump, and another located at the barnyard, equipped with a type of iron pump that was hooked up and operated by wind power through a tall windmill. The pumped water was put into a large vat trough for the cattle, horses, and other animals to drink.

In regard to the barnyard, I should mention what a sight it was in the winter time to see all the horses and cattle of mixed breeds and many colors all milling around contentedly, munching corn fodder and drinking fresh water.

The foregoing paragraphs give one an idea of the buildings and pumps used to carry forth the operation of farming in Sassafras Neck in the period we are writing about. I'll now explain how the land of each farm was divided up, tilled, and rotated crop wise.

Each farm was divided up into five different fields, with exception to small hog lots, poultry yards, orchards, and vegetable gardens or truck patches. The five-field system that prevailed for many years (up until recent years, or from 1950 to the early 1980s) was referred to as a rotating system in which crops were changed from one of the five fields to the other every year. For instance, a farm is in complete till as follows for one farm for one year: one field is plowed and corn is planted, two fields are plowed and wheat is planted in late summer and early fall, one field is in hay, one in pasture, and one in fallow, meaning land in rest. (People used to believe in resting the land.) In the second year after the corn is harvested, the field is re-plowed and wheat is planted and referred to as stalk-ground wheat. Then, the third year the same field becomes the fallow wheat field. The fourth year it becomes pasture land and in five years it is back into corn again.

This cycle of tillage, as you see, occurs to all five fields in an alternating pattern. Usually, timothy seed and clover seed were sewn in the fallow ground wheat field, and later when mature growth was reached in summer, it was cut and stored for hay.

We will now see how a year of tillage was carried out, say from the late 1880s up to the 1920s. Winter has come and gone, the spring or late winter thaw has occurred, and it is about mid-March: It has begun to warm up, but windy March days make it feel cool. The horses are turned out of the barnyard into the open pasture field to run, kick up their heels, and get rid of their excess energy after being penned up in the barnyard all winter, and to shape up for work.

Work starts with the barnyard manure being forked up, hauled out, and spread on the pasture field. Around the first of April, the pasture field is plowed up by horse drawn hand, or walking plows, usually pulled by three horses. According to the size of the farm, one, two, or even three such plows would be used, one man to each plow. The plowing would be followed by dicing or by harrowing to cut or break up the plowed furrows until the soil was in good granular texture. Some farmers would be ready to plant corn in the latter part of April; some did not plant until May. Some did not plant until the sign in the Farmer's Almanac was right, yet others liked to hear the call of the whip-poor-will bird before planting.

Before the coming in of the farm tractor, all corn was planted by a planting machine drawn by two horses. The discs and harrows took normally five horses to pull them over the ground. So, the corn is planted and in a couple of weeks, starts to come up. After being up for a couple of weeks, it gets cultivated to ward off the oncoming minute weeds. Back in the 1850s up to approximately 1900s, cultivating was all done by one-man hand cultivators drawn by one horse. In later years, the two-horse riding cultivators were used, allowing a man to sit on a seat instead of having to walk. Usually, the young corn was cultivated at least twice before it grew too high to get through. So now we are finished with the corn for a while until late summer and fall harvest.

The next operation to come along in later June was the mowing down and storing of the hay crop for the feeding of the horses and cows in winter. The sweet clover and the timothy hay, when mowed, made a pleasant aroma across the countryside in the early summer. After the hay was mowed, it was raked up into wind rows, loaded into hay wagons, hauled to the stable, and stored in the big open loft.

In early days, this was all done by hand and foot. The hay would be tramped down by foot to pack it as it was being unloaded into the loft. Sometimes, when the loft wouldn't hold all the hay, it would be put into a stack (haystack) along the outer area of the barnyard. In later years, in the mechanical farm machine era, hay was put into bales by mechanical balers so it could be handled much easier for storing or stacking.

At this stage, the hay is in and now we are into wheat harvest. In the early days of my life, this was a three-phase operation for two fields of wheat and was performed in the months of July and into August. The wheat, ripe and golden in color, was a beautiful site, especially when the wind was up, as it would make the grain wave and ripple like a golden sea.

First, the wheat was cut by a reaper and binding machine drawn by five horses and operated by one man on horse to guide the horses. The wheat would be bound up into sheaves (by the machine) then two men would walk behind, gather up these sheaves, and set them up into shocks of about a dozen or so sheaves, then top them off with two cap-sheaves to withstand the weather (rain). This then was a shock of wheat, so a field then had a few hundred shocks according to the size of the field.

The second operation was to gather up all the shocks by loading all the sheaves onto wagons and then hauling them to a convenient spot where they were unloaded and put into large stacks to better withstand the weather and wait until a threshing rig would come to thresh the wheat. In my younger days, there were only two threshing rigs to serve the west end of Sassafras Neck. They were powered by large steam engines mounted on a heavy tractor type frame with four wheels and were self-propelled (only slowly). They towed the threshing machine itself from farm to farm. A long canvas and fiber belt running over the main pulley of the engine to the main pulley of the threshing machine furnished power to thresh wheat or other grain.

Every farmer had to get a supply of bituminous coal (soft coal) to fire the engine boiler and they had to haul water from a river, creek, or stream (whichever was closest) for the boiler to make steam to power the engine. Sheaves of wheat were dropped in the front of the thresher to become straw and wheat grain at the other end. The separated grain ran down a chute at the end of which it would be bagged up into two bushel bags (120 pounds). The straw would be blown out the back of the thresher into two or three large piles. This straw would be used in wintertime to bed down the barnyards and to become manure for the following spring to be plowed under corn ground. The threshing phase of wheat harvest was a big operation done with big combine machines.

There was an old-time spirit of fellowship and good neighbor relations woven through all of this back in those days that is gone now, but worth remembering. In earlier days, the farmers of each neck within Sassafras Neck joined together in good spirit, with their men, wagons, and horses, to help one another. On, say, a three-hundred-acre farm, it would take a crew of twenty-six to thirty men, six to ten wagons, and twelve to twenty horses. Since the average farmer only owned two to three wagons, they would have to work together.

The threshed wheat was stored in the barn loft or was hauled to the nearest wharf and loaded on a schooner to be transported to Baltimore and put into big storage silos until it could be sold to buyers. Wheat threshing was also a big operation for farmers' wives, daughters, and neighbor women, who had to feed twenty-five to thirty men breakfast, dinner, and supper. Farmers' wives also joined to help one another for wheat harvesting and threshing. Hams would be gotten out of the meat house and boiled, old hens would be killed for chicken pot-pie, and there would be kettles full of new potatoes, heads of new cabbage to be boiled in ham liquor, new beets, slaw, and new peas, all from the vegetable garden planted back in April, milk cans full of iced tea and lemonade with chunks of ice and, of course, coffee. A thresh dinner table was a sight to see and a better one to taste. There were always plenty of leftovers for supper. Breakfast always consisted of hotcakes and sausage, or ham and eggs.

Of the twenty-five to thirty men, several might be Negroes. In those days, the Negro men ate at a separate table to themselves, but with the same kind and amount of food. The Negroes at the time we are writing about did not expect, or indeed, did not want to eat at the same table as the whites, but there was never any animosity over this. That, I guess, was segregation, but oddly enough the black and white people seemed to have love, caring and much respect for each other. In fact, everyone in the west end of Sassafras Neck were good friends and neighbors to one another in times of trouble.

This good neighborly attitude does not prevail in modern times in Sassafras Neck or any other neck or community. Times have changed much and so have people.

After wheat harvest, it is somewhere around the middle of August and there are a few days left before the start of the corn harvest. During this little interval, most of the farmers took the time to straighten up their hedgerows out along the sides and small banks of country roads. This was done by cutting down the weeds, vines, and other trash vegetation. The hedge trimmings would be piled up and burned and a pleasant odor would waft across the countryside.

About this time of the year, bees, or yellow-jackets, would be starting to nest up along the hedgerows for the winter. The hedgerow work would occasionally stir up a nest of these bees here and there and men would stomp, flail with their hats, cuss, and even run to keep from being stung by these nasty little insects. The cleaning up and trimming of the hedgerow was done by hand with a bramble scythe (a long bladed hedge knife) and fork to pile up the brush. Hedgerows that had grown up between the fields were mostly left alone, as they made good shelter for birds like quail, doves and songbirds and small animals such as the skunk, opossum, rabbit, woodchuck, quail, and a vicious little animal known as the weasel.

By the first of September or a little later, the corn is tall and green and ready to start turning brown, the corn silk is drying up and the ears of corn are starting to sag down the stalk. It's time to start harvesting corn. This, as with wheat, is a three-phase operation and in some cases four. However, it commences with the cutting and shocking of corn stalks.

Corn was planted in rows three feet apart, with hills of corn measuring three feet apart down the row. So there were four hills of corn in a three-foot square, with (after thinning down) two stalks of corn in each hill. The shock rows were the width of two corn rows, and corn from sixteen rows on either side of the shock row would be cut and set up to form the shock. The shocks would be tied near the top with one stalk of corn keeping the shock together and straight. The result was eventually a corn field with rows and rows of corn shocks across the entire field.

Much of the cutting and shocking of the corn was done by the black migrant workers from Virginia. These black people would live with the native blacks while working in the Sassafras Neck area. The migrant black people ate foods from the country stores such as slabs of cheese, soda crackers, canned beans, sardines, sour pickles, bread, dried chipped beef, and potted tongue.

After corn cutting for the neck farmers was completed, the workers would migrate on to other areas of the Eastern Shore of Maryland and into Delaware. The corn in the shock will set until it eventually dries in the shock for husking out when dry and brittle. While this is taking place, the ground between the shock rows is plowed, and the stock ground wheat is sown. The fallow ground wheat has already been sown during the July wheat harvest.

After the stock ground wheat has been sown, the corn is ready to husk out of the shock. So, from each shock the ears of corn are husked out and piled up into piles in the shock rows to dry out and air cure the ears. The fodder stalks are tied up into bundles (sheaves) and stood up into large fodder shocks. When the corn in the piles has dried a little, the corn is hauled to the grain barn and put in the cribs; some will be used to feed the cattle and horses in winter, some to fatten hogs and to feed poultry, some to grind for cornmeal, and some to be sold. To complete the corn harvest, the fodder will be hauled to the barnyard and stacked up atop the corn shed and near the barnyard. This completes the plowing, planting, and harvesting of crops for the year.

There was another important phase of farming that went on all year round. This was the raising and maintaining of a herd of milk cows (or dairy cows, if you will.) According to the size of the farm, these herds would consist of anywhere between ten to thirty cows, plus one or two bulls. They were milked in the morning and again in the evening. This was a monthly source of cash money for the farmers, which they greatly depended upon, as many times they did not reap great profits from the grain crops due to a bad growing year, fertilizer bills, and poor market prices. Also, with the cows, oftentimes a calf would be born and what they did not keep to raise, they sold for veal.

Up until about the late 1930s, the milk would be collected and processed for shipment by nearby creameries and sent to Philadelphia, PA or Wilmington, DE by railroad tank cars. For many years, creameries operated in Cecilton and in Massey, over the river in Kent County, where milk was processed into cheese which would be shipped by rail.

I have related this chapter to farming as it was in my own lifetime, in the period from 1912 to the late 1930s, at which point World War II and other events took place to change farming all around. In the late 1920s, some of the owners of the larger farms started to use the gasoline tractor to pull the plows and other equipment. At about the same time, large gasoline tractors were being used rather than old steam engines to power the threshing machines. The first gas tractor to be used by the Sassafras Neck farmers was the little Fordons manufactured by the Ford Motor Company. Then came the International Farmall, followed by the Allis Chalmers, and the small John Deere with the horizontal engine. By the 1930s, very few farmers were using horses for pulling power.

Another phase of the farming operation headed up by the farmer's wife in most cases, was the poultry raising and egg and butter operation. In late winter, choice eggs from the hens' nests were held back to set under the hens to be hatched, which would be the new crop of chickens for that particular year. It was a good sight to see the fuzzy, wee chicks hatched out at Easter each year. Chickens were the main poultry crop, but many farms raised some tame geese and Muscovy or Peking ducks. Most farms had a flock of guineas, which always seemed to be half wild as they laid eggs and hatched them way out in the thorn hedgerows, coming to the farmyard occasionally to eat some grain. In later years, many turkeys were also raised for table food.

The farmer's wife also made the butter. Milk was put into an upright sort of tank called a separator, which means it separated the cream from the milk. When enough cream was separated, it was put in a churn to make butter. The churns were the hand-cranked type. When patted out and put into molds to make exactly a pound, the butter was then wrapped in a special wax paper and was a pretty golden color. Some of the butter was made into balls and put in a pickle brine and stored in stoneware crocks for winter use. The butter that was not needed for the table went to the country store, along with the excess eggs, and would be traded for groceries such as tea, coffee, sugar, spices, and other types of goods.

Most of the farms, in my earlier boyhood days, also had orchards of apples, pears, and peaches. They were picked up and the women folk canned, preserved, and made jams and jellies for winter use. When I was a boy, considerable amounts of fruit would be packed in baskets and hauled to the nearest wharf and be shipped to produce markets in Baltimore, Wilmington, and Philadelphia.

To sum up this chapter, one can get an idea of how the land was handled, cared for, and farmed in a way that was good, even biblical in nature. Sadly it is no longer the way we see it farmed today.

With the five field rotation method of farming, one field or one-fifth of the land of any farm laid fallow and rested; in the modern way of tillage, all of the land is plowed up year after year and there is no such thing as fallow ground. Modern big operation tilling of land is full of greed for all that can be sown, raised, and harvested and people today think "to hell with the fallowing" or resting of the land.

But the Bible mentions fallowing or fallow ground several times. Reference for a good plan of fallow can be found in Leviticus, Chapter 25, verses one through six.

Steam powered wheat threshing c1920 in Cecilton (Catherine Short/Cecil College)

Windmill used for pumping well water

VINCENT TAYLOR

CHAPTER VI
HUNTING, FISHING AND TRAPPING

Many of the people of the west end of Sassafras Neck were very fond of hunting, fishing, and trapping, for both the sport of it and the monetary profit from it; yet for others, it was a bread and butter activity.

Many of the west end residents (whether farmer or villager) owned and kept rabbit dogs. They were not the present day popular beagles, but a type of rabbit dog that was somewhat larger yet was marked similar to the beagle—often referred to as the "rabbit hound."

In my earlier years rabbits were plentiful, as woods were better kept, hedgerows were not uprooted, and the creeks and rivers were not overrun with pleasure boats.

Around the middle of November, the hunting season would start for rabbits. Off went the hunters with their dogs and ten and twelve gauge shotguns, mostly single barrel, a few double barrel, and a few pump or automatic guns that were used about fifty or more years ago. For several days all up and down the countryside the baying of dogs and guns going off could be heard.

One could smell fresh rabbit being cooked by the women folk. Some favored parboiling the rabbit meat tender and then slightly browning it so that a flavorful gravy could be made for mashed potatoes. Others cooked the rabbit carcass with bread crumbs, onions, celery and juice, then added potatoes and dumplings for a pot-pie. Then again, a few would stuff the rabbit carcass with bread crumbs, onions, and celery (dressing) and then bake the rabbit. One of my uncles would not eat rabbit in this fashion as they reminded him of cats laying in the roaster.

Many rabbits used to abound in the creek marshes. They had black feet and were a little larger than the woods or hedgerow rabbit. Many times when hunting for rabbits, quail would jump up out of the hedgerows or the brush piles. Squirrels used to be plentiful as well and were hunted and cooked about the same way as the rabbits. The quail would also be cooked along with the rabbit or squirrel if parboiled. Dove hunting in the fall of the year was also good sport. The yellow leg plover used to be plentiful as well, but not as much in recent years.

Many people in the early fall would also hunt the ground hog, or woodchuck for table game. Many would not though because of the strong gamey taste, however, if a young chuck was roasted in the right way with onions, celery, and other special seasonings along with sweet potatoes, it was good eating. Many of the black folks were very fond of woodchuck and opossum cooked in the same manner.

In the early fall, hunters would go to the marshes to hunt the rail-bird (no more in the west end marshes) which was rather a long legged bird with a fairly long bill and skinny body. Mostly the breast of the bird was cooked and had an odd marshy taste, but wasn't too bad.

My father liked to hunt and eat these birds when, for a while, he farmed land bordering on Pearce Creek in Pearce Neck. (He turned to farming when he was told by the family doctor to get out of the smoke and dust of the blacksmith shop). The best hunting in the creeks were the wild ducks, such as the Mallard, Pintail, Blue Bills, Black Ducks, and some Canvas Back (fall and winter ducks) and Wood Ducks, and Teal (summer ducks).

Fifty or so years ago, almost all farmers had a flat bottom boat called a bateau, which was fourteen to sixteen feet long. At that time, one could row or skull up the creek guts into marshes and get in some good shooting sport, and also some good eating. Someone who lived along a riverfront or bay shore would usually erect a blind from the marsh grasses and hedges and set out a flock of wood decoys in hopes to toll in some Canvas Back ducks from out in the head of the bay after they had been stirred up by the hunters over on the Susquehanna Flats. Many of the hunters owned a Chesapeake Bay Retriever, which would retrieve the ducks that were shot off the bay shore.

Wild geese were not as prevalent back then as they are now, due to the fact that there is approximately five or more times more corn grown now than there used to be and there is more gleanings for game birds of all kinds. However, some geese did arrive and even in those days many were taken and very much relished by the neck people.

Some of the people of Sassafras Neck loved the sport of fox hunting on off days in late fall and during the winter (like the old song "When the work is done next fall.") Fox hunting was done purely for sport. Many folks owned foxhounds. Indeed, a few had packs of hounds. Sometimes as many as twelve to twenty hunters could be seen chasing foxes across fields, through the woods, on the country dirt roads, and sometimes up farm lanes right on up to and throughout the farm yard; pounding hooves, hollering, shouting and barking dogs could be heard for miles. It was a great sight to see and lots of fun—more so, I suspect, than the booted, red coated gentry type of fox hunt.

When the fall and winter hunting are done for the season, there is the snapping turtle (if one likes him) early in the spring that comes out of the main creek, goes up into the smaller streams and into the plowed ground and lays eggs in a dug out hollow nest. Some folks would catch these snappers, butcher them for eating, and even eat the eggs. After being butchered, the meat was put in a pot with onions, potatoes, and celery for snapper pot-pie. Others would make snapper soup. Many of these snappers could be found in the marsh mud flats and were brought up from out of the mud by using a steel rod with a hook bent on one end. One could see a hole in the mud wherein the snapper was and could hook it with this steel rod and pulled up out of the mud. This was hard, dirty hunting. Many small Red-Belly Terrapins were taken out of the marshes, cleaned, then cut up and fried like chicken—which was very good eating. Leading hotels and restaurants in the nearby towns and cities, especially Baltimore, would buy these snappers and terrapins and bill them on their menus as delicacies.

Now, at around the end of May just as green wheat is beginning to head, we would hear a sound at night that sounded like, "bar-ra-rum," over and over, which was the mating call of the male bullfrog to the female bullfrog. Many of us young fellows used to hunt these frogs from out of a rowboat with a flashlight. One man would row or pole the boat and the other man was the frog catcher. When the frog hollers, his head and eyes stick up out of the water. With the flashlight turned toward him, his eyes will shine and he will stay there sort of mesmerized by the light. The boat is poled toward the frog and the catcher in the bow of the boat quickly grabs him and put him in a crate in the boat. I used to like this sport. Sometimes we would catch from three to five dozen, which we would sell to buyers. Once in a while we would have cooked frog legs to eat, but mostly we sold them, and there again, many of them wound up in cities at the leading hotels and restaurants. From the foregoing, one can get an idea of what and how we hunted in the Sassafras Neck area.

Let's now talk about some of the trapping activities. In the west end of the neck, many hunters trapped for the muskrat in the marshes and other animals in the woods and hedgerows. Muskrats in the river and creek marshes were fairly plentiful years ago. The trapping season would usually start in late December and last through the winter into March. This was very hard and very cold work, slogging around through the marshes in hip boots, carrying twenty to thirty pounds of steel traps plus an ax, knife, gun, and stakes.

Most of the trappers were a tough, wiry, weathered bunch of men. Many times in late January and February, the rivers, creeks, and marshes would freeze up and when this occurred, it put a stop to trapping until around the first of March. But with all the hardships, most made a few dollars in the muskrat season. I can remember one winter my father trapped the Pearce Creek marsh and had a very good season in the winter of 1919-1920, getting four dollars for a brown hide and four dollars and fifty cents for a black hide. Not everyone, but many cooked and ate the muskrat carcasses. As the muskrat's main food is the root of the cattail marsh plant called Calmus Root, it gave the meat a very special flavor. I myself, my elders, and my own children all liked to eat muskrat parboiled and browned with onions and celery.

Due to many developments and changes in Sassafras Neck, very few muskrats are caught anymore. Much farmland in the river, creek, and marsh areas has been bought up by out of state people, strangers, and land speculating syndicates. They immediately post NO TRESPASSING signs all around their acquired property. However, a few are still being trapped in season. I manage to get two or three carcasses in the winter time, and they make a good dish for me, as my wife knows how to cook them really well.

In the woods it used to be that raccoons, fox, skunks, weasels, opossum, and occasionally a mink or an otter, would be trapped. During and after World War I, fur was in great demand and sold for a good price, as women wanted muskrat coats, fur wraps, and neck pieces, and many stylish men were wearing raccoon coats.

A few of the real old-timers would trap rabbits by setting snare traps—four or five wood pegs driven in the ground in a circle shape, eight to ten inches in diameter with a "Y" shaped peg in the middle, then a straight stick with one end punched in an apple and laid over the "Y" peg, and the other end affixed to a trigger arrangement. A sapling would be bent over, strong twine tied to the bent over end, and the other end of the twine looped around the circle of pegs and hooked in to the trigger stick. When the rabbit bit the apple it flipped the trigger toggle and the loop of twine flipped right up around the rabbit's neck as the sapling sprang back, thus hanging mister rabbit.

Many young boys that grew up were taught how to trap by their fathers, older brothers, or grandfathers. They were also taught the identity of major tree species, wild plants for greens and medical purposes, and many other practical things. Due to many factors and the changing times, I believe this sort of instruction does not occur too often today which, I think, is rather sad.

Let us now turn to the fishing business in the bay, river, creek areas, and the head of the bay where large pound nets were set up and fished. Pound netting was quite a big fishing operation some years ago, even up until the 1930s.

A pound net was a large net in the shape of a fence, and square in shape on the outer fence area. The netting was hung and supported on large poles stuck deep down into the bay or river bottom. Leading into the square part of the net was a funnel shaped section of netting referred to as the heart. The part of the net just described was set way out in the river near the channels. Then, from the pound and funnel, a long straight piece of net was stretched almost into shore, and was also supported on poles. Fish would run or follow along this straight stretch of net called hedging right into the funnel section, and were trapped or penned within the impounding square area. Hence, the term "pound net." After being trapped, the fish were dipped out and put into a scow to be towed to buyer locations across the bay at Havre de Grace, North East, and Betterton. This type of net was set specifically to catch the runs of shad fish and herring that came up the bay in the spring to spawn in the fresh river waters at the head of the bay. Of course, other kinds of fish were caught in the pound nets including rockfish, perch, bass, catfish, and even many eels.

In those days, the fish traders or peddlers would line up at the various roads leading to the fishing shores to buy direct from the fisherman. They would peddle fish to all of the country sides and villages in Sassafras Neck, and even peddle fish over in Delaware. They peddled in horse and wagon rigs, and later on were using Model-T Fords. In the spring, when pound fishing was in operation, one could smell fried fish being cooked in all the towns and villages. Many people used to salt down from two hundred to as many as a thousand herring for winter use in wooden tubs and barrels, according to the size of the family.

Years ago, the Sassafras, Bohemia, and Elk Rivers would have many pound nets set up in them, but now-a-days there are very few. So many pleasure boats in recent years have just about driven the fish out of the creeks and rivers according to the watermen. A fisherman friend of mine told me that in some of the marshes some of the cattails even seem to be dying due to probable pollution from dozens upon dozens of pleasure craft in the Sassafras River alone. At this time, it would be hard to say just where all the boat pleasure business will all wind up or how the US Conservation Department and State Government will deal with it.

In years gone by, fishermen from Tilghman's Island would come up the bay and set up and fish pound nets. The Charles Sinclair outfit (Sinclair is now deceased) used to set pound nets off shore out in head of the bay from a long bar of sandy shore referred to as Hazelmore, between Ponds Creek, Pearce Creek, and Grove Point. Also, the Harrison outfit from Tilghman's Island set pound nets off shore adjacent to the mouth of the Elk River, between Reybolds Wharf and Cabin John Creek. Harrison processed most of his herring catch right on the shore. He had a fish-cleaning building and a pickling plant on the shore. Just about all of the many fishing shores have now become trailer camp sites, housing developments, estate properties, or marina areas.

There was still another fishing operation carried on in the creek, mostly by individuals who, in many cases, were the winter trappers switching over to creek fishing when trapping season was over. These fellows set up a type of net called a fike net, which could be set and fished by one man. The fike was merely netting fastened around wooden hoops made of hickory wood, and inside was a series of funnel netting sections, through which the fish would enter and not be able to escape. This fike was a very efficient one-man net.

Another type of net used in the open water areas of the creeks and rivers was the gill net. This net was made of twine with square meshes, was anywhere from two hundred to seven hundred feet in length, and was four, six, or eight feet in depth or width, and suspended in the water by corks. The net hung in the water, the narrow measurement vertical, and caught the fish by the gills; they were then taken out of the net by hand. These lone wolf type fishermen peddled their catch around the countryside to the local people. They also sold some to buyers.

We cannot close this chapter without mention of yet another altogether different kind of "fisherman"—the eagle and the osprey. Osprey, being commonly called fish hawks, and smaller creek hawks such as duck hawks, were very numerous, and the arrival of the fish hawk heralded the coming in of the shad fish and herring in the spring of the year. The bald eagles used to chase the fish hawks up into the sky and go nearly out of sight, and eventually the fish hawk would drop the fish it had caught and the eagle would dive through the air and catch it before it landed back into the water. I can remember a fish hawk nest in a tall dead tree on Rose Hill Farm in Grove Neck that was used by these hawks for many, many years before the tree finally fell in recent years. These beautiful birds, for the most part, are just about all gone from the upper bay and the Sassafras Neck area, suffering the same fate as the fish, game, and other wildlife, crowded out by too many people, boats, commotion, and pollution.

Many years ago (forty, more or less) the Corps of Engineers Baltimore District took over all of Pearce Creek, dammed up the mouth of it, and made a spill area for mud, muck, and other types of river bottom material which was dredged up from the bay ship channel from Poole's Island into the Elk River, thus destroying one of the finest fish and wildlife areas at the head of the bay, and somewhat later did just about the same thing at Cabin John Creek, just up Elk River from Reybolds Wharf. Later the Corps tried to grab Pond Creek for a spoil area, but the property owners in that area fought against it and won; at least for the time being, thank God.

Another small creek in the mouth of the Sassafras River suffered the same fate as Pearce Creek and Cabin John Creek a few years back to accommodate more channel dredging spoils. In this writer's opinion, some of the activities and proposals of the Corps of Engineers is very questionable; why should all of the good areas be sacrificed for the sake of the big ship owners and labeled "progress"? This is just another type of activity that has degraded the once beautiful west end of Sassafras Neck. No doubt, much degradation is yet to come and will be labeled as progress.

Rose Hill

Crew of a pound-net skiff tending a pound-net on the Chesapeake Bay c 1940. Photographer unknown. Courtesy Collection of the Chesapeake Bay Maritime Museum St. Michaels, Md.

CHAPTER VII
THE TRADESMEN

The blacksmith shop and wheelwright shop in the village of Earleville and the carpenters and painters will be described in this chapter. We will start with the blacksmith shops. Well back in the 1800s, my great-grandfather Taylor operated a blacksmith shop at Grindstone Corner, which was where Grove Neck Road and the Pond's Neck Road branched off from one another. This was reported to be the first blacksmith in the west end of the Neck. Then later his son, my grandfather Taylor, operated a shop in the village of Earleville. Even later, also in Earleville, grandfather Taylor, with two of his sons (one of which was my father) bought a two-story building and continued blacksmithing and wheelwrighting and repairing farm equipment and wagons.

This was about the greatest height of this business, and at the time my brother and I were just small boys. My uncle and my father could both do any phase of the work, but Uncle Jonny mostly did the iron work, and my father specialized in wood work for wagons, harrows and wheel work, etc. They both shod horses.

Just before my grandfather closed his old shop to open a new one with his sons at the new location, he was tragically struck by lightning and killed during a severe electrical storm one afternoon. However, the new shop thrived for many years afterward, until the automobile, farm tractor, and mechanized equipment put most of the blacksmith shops out of business.

At one end of the shop the forge for the heating of iron was set up. It was made of brick with a fire basin and a chimney and was piped into a bellows nearby, which was turned by a hand crank to force air into the fire basin to make a hot fire. Often my brother and I would turn or crank the forge bellows as it was being heated. The fire was used to heat iron for blacksmithing and the shaping of iron, which was done on a big anvil near the forge. Other equipment for blacksmithing entailed a hand operated drill for the drilling of iron, a work bench with a big vise mounted on it, and many tongs and other hand tools used to perform the work, plus a large tub filled with water to cool the hot iron when needed.

One of the big iron working jobs was shoeing horses. That was the fitting and nailing on of iron horse shoes to the horse's hooves, and these were mostly the horses that pulled family carriages, or riding horses referred to as driving horses.

Most every family had a driving horse either on the farm or in the villages or small towns. The horses, one or two at a time, were brought into the shop and haltered to a big ring-belt which was set into one of the shop frame timbers. This area of the shop had a dirt floor. The correct size of iron horse shoes would be selected out of the various kegs, then put into the forge to be heated red hot to be shaped on the anvil to perfectly fit each horse's hoof. The horse's hooves would be cleaned off before fitting took place. The new horse shoes would be nailed on with a special kind of nail made only for that purpose.

Many a kid and some men would bend these nails around a round piece of iron and make a horse shoe ring, which they would wear until the bright silver shine wore off. My brother and I made dozens of these rings for our buddies. There was a special piece of equipment made of a horse's tail which was mounted onto a wood handle and swished over the horses in the summer to keep the flies off while they were being haltered and shod. Many times the owners would give us boys a nickel for doing this. If any horse manure was dropped in the shop it would be shoveled off to one side to be used later in the family garden.

Another big phase of the iron work was the cutting of steel tires for the various wood wagon, buggy, and carriage wheels. After much wear, steel tires got loose from expansion, so they were measured by a wheel compass for circumference, then cut and made smaller, and re-forged and welded. Then the whole tire was heated to expand it so that it could be put on the wheel rims to shrink tight, and then the tire was belted to the rim, making the entire wheel solid. When only one small carriage tire was involved it would be heated in the forge. Many times, four to eight heavy wagon wheel tires would be made ready to put back on the wood wheels. In this case a bunch of steel tires would be laid on the ground in a stack. Kindling wood soaked with coal oil would be laid around the wheels and then set afire, thus expanding the steel tires. Also, the wood wheels would be repaired as needed with new spokes, a piece of new rim, or a whole new rim. There was always a can of red paint in the shop used to paint any new wood repair work.

The blacksmith also repaired iron anchors, hooks, grappling irons, and other things for the pound-fisherman. They repaired and even made new lengths of chain for farmers and others, made iron hinges for large farm gates, and sharpened many tools of various kinds.

In the other end of the shop, most of the wood-working took place. A stationary gasoline engine sat on a mount to power a band-saw and a bench type rip-saw. Another work bench with a vise and many sorts of wood-working hand tools was also situated in this end of the shop. A supply of oak lumber from the local saw mills was on hand and pieces would be sawed out to make and repair wagons, harrows, clod rollers, and single, double, triple, four, and even five horse pulling bars which were generally referred to as single trees, double trees, etc.

In the heyday of the blacksmith and wheelwright shop it was all a sight to see and hear—with black smoke billowing from the soft coal used in the forge, the bellows moaning, the anvil ringing, and Uncle Jonny singing diddy-type songs while he was working at the forge and anvil. In the other end of the shop, the bark of the stationary engine (it has a make and break type of magnet firing system) and the whine and buzzing of the saws made yet another bunch of sounds.

Two salesmen from large hardware and supply companies used to come by once a month. One was from R. W. Norris Co. in Baltimore, MD, and the other was from the Herbert Hearn Hardware Co. in Cambridge, MD. New wheel hubs, spokes, rims, iron for tires, belts, nails, horse shoes, tools, and welding compounds would be ordered from the salesmen as needed and would be shipped by steam boat to the wharf at Fredericktown, MD.

Many people would be in and out of the shop every day and many would wait if they were getting a horse shod or a small repair job done. Sometimes there would be three, four, or more at a time, especially on a rainy day. Most knew one another, so they would have a good time talking and telling stories, chewing tobacco and spitting all over the place. Once in a while, one might have a pint or so of whiskey (more often "white mule bootleg") in which case they would all have a drink. Now one can imagine what it was like back in the days of the country blacksmith shop.

Now let's take a look at the carpentry trade in Sassafras Neck. There were different classes of carpenters—very fine mechanics who built houses of all types and even churches, and the barn and stable builders of special types of framing who were good mechanics with saw, broad ax, plane, chisels, steel nails, and of course hammer and hatchet. In those days there were no power tools, only hand tools were used. Also most of the carpenters could lay brick chimneys, stone and brick foundations, and plaster walls and ceilings.

There were real craftsmen who had tremendous pride in their work and finished product. Many of these men inherited the trade from their elders and handed it down to their sons up into the 1920s, but after World War I this began to change. Previous to the 1920s it would take half a dozen carpenters plus two or three apprentices four to six months and even up to a year (according to size) to build a house or a large barn or stable. Most of the larger houses were two stories with a sizable attic, a main stairway to the second story front rooms, another leading to the second story back rooms usually going up out of the kitchen, and a third stairway going to the second story to the attic. Many times the roof had dormer window framing.

Generally, the farmhouses had a front and back porch.

The average working class of people today have much smaller houses, mostly all being on one floor; some are referred to as ranch houses. Many of the old barn and stable farm buildings that were built before my day were still in use in this time we are writing about, but in recent years, (the 1960s, 70s, and 80s) many have been torn down, burned down, or otherwise destroyed.

Most of the barns and stables built back in the 1800s were all framed with hand hewn timber from the local woods and put together with the mortise and peg type of joints, all of which would be laid out on the ground, fabricated, then raised or erected and joined and pinned a piece at a time. Most of these old time carpenters were old men when I was a boy. Siding and floor planks came from the local saw mills.

In my day a few barns were built, and also stables, but with lumber from the local saw mills and lumber yards. The lumber yard that served the needs of the people in Sassafras Neck in my day was Woodall's Lumber Yard just down over the river in Kent County at Georgetown. This fine old lumber, farm, and building supply company was finally purchased by Baugh Fertilizer Co. of Baltimore. In recent years and at present (1981) it has become a town marina.

The type of old time craftsmen that we have talked about in this chapter do not exist in modern times. There was one type of carpenter, who usually worked with another carpenter as a pair, building small additions to houses, sheds, poultry houses, outdoor toilets, meat houses, and repair work in the village, town, and countryside. This was somewhat a rougher type of carpentry and did not require the finesse of the professional house carpenter. These carpenters, however, also did good, solid, substantial work and took pride in what they could do. In fact, they were much in demand, because the top notch men only wanted to work and apply their skills to the larger, more complicated types of buildings.

Last, but not least, were the hatchet and saw kind of workmen. They were found here and there in Sassafras Neck, and could be classed as handymen. They built quite a few hog pens, which were made of heavy saw mill planks and timbers, and had to be made stout to hold as many as eight to ten hogs for fattening up in the fall. They could also do repair work to sheds, stables, and barns. Back in the days of rotation, tilling, and crop farming, many large field and barnyard gates were needed to contain horses and cattle in one field or another. These large gates were made of heavy saw mill boards, put together with belts, and hung onto the gate posts with heavy iron hinges made in the blacksmith shop. The gate posts were of large diameter locust or cedar wood as they lasted in the ground a long time without rotting. On these posts were hung a heavy gauge page wire (steel) usually three to four feet height, and two runs of barbed wire would be stretched and nailed above the page wire making the total height of the fence about five feet high.

Some of the hatchet and saw men did a lot of fencing, as all five fields of a farm were kept fenced all around their perimeters, except where the hedgerows grew up and served as fences. However, the fence on a large farm could run a couple more miles. Farm fences now-a-days have about gone out of style because horses are not used, and for the most part very few dairy herds of cattle exist on the present farm land. Most of the fences and hedgerows have been ripped up and done away with, running all the small wild animals, quail, dove, and birds out of house and home.

To get back to the hand type of carpenter, many of them could build a decent looking scow and also row boats, and many did. Speaking of boat building, there used to be a family of people in Fredericktown that built a lot of the better large type of boats. One of their specialties was the boat used by some of the upper bay fisherman, referred to as the Gilling Skiff. This was a round bottom boat 22 feet to 25 feet in length, and a very fine looking, seaworthy boat. Like the Chesapeake Bay Skipjack, they are mostly all gone today.

There were a few men who painted of houses, barns, stables, and other types of buildings and the sheet metal roofs of barns and stables. Not much painting was done on the inside of the houses because most people used wallpaper on the walls and ceilings, which was done for the most part by the women folk. The inside wood trim did, however, get painted, but not often as paint was then of a much better substance (lead, linseed oil, turpentine, and color pigments) and stayed on much longer than present day paints.

Even though farming was the backbone of the Sassafras Neck economy, there were always enough other types of work resulting from it that kept just about every man employed one way or another.

It is too bad that these types of rural communities do not exist today, but again, how could they with all the big business, big operators, big politics and government, and shifting multitudes of people in these contemporary times?

At one time in the past and even into my lifetime unemployment in Sassafras Neck was unheard of. So from the foregoing writing of this chapter, one can gather and understand how the people of Sassafras Neck worked and made their living by none other than agriculture, farming, fishing, or trapping. To wind up this chapter, it could be mentioned that there was very little, if any, class distinction between the people as a whole. Well off farmers or businessmen were as friendly to farm laborers and black people as they were to everyone else.

Blacksmith Shop

CHAPTER VIII
HOG KILLING TIME

There was a popular country Sassafras neck tradition we called "hog-killing." Early in the fall of the year, the hogs (many of which were little pigs during the past winter) were rounded up out of the hog lots, orchards, and meadows and put into the hog pen so that they could be fattened up on the fresh corn that was now being husked or as some would say, shucked out. The hogs being penned up could not run their fat off and by Thanksgiving those hogs would weigh from 250 to 300 pounds on average.

In Earleville, the village folks usually had two hogs per family. The farmers would have anywhere from six to twelve hogs per farm family. While penned up, the hogs would have a "swill" to drink along with the corn, and of course, fresh water. The "swill" came from the "slop barrel" which just about everyone had. The slop consisted of a mixture of vegetable tops, potato peelings, fruit peelings, stale bread, and sour milk and cream. This would be poured in the trough in the pen and the hogs loved it. Hogs also (before they were penned up) liked to chomp the fallen apples and pears in the orchards. After much gorging of food, by Thanksgiving they would be ready for butchering, which took place between Thanksgiving and Christmas in the frosty weather.

In the down neck, or West End area, lived a fellow and his two sons, and they conducted the business of killing hogs. The main requirement in the way of special equipment was a hog scalder. This was a large elongated tub made of heavy oak planks and covered with sheet iron. The scalder would be set up over a trench dug in the ground in an appropriate spot. Then a wood fire would be lit in the trench under the scalder. A pipe stack was arranged in one end to make the fire burn good to heat the water in the scalder to near boiling point.

Many men were needed at a large hog-killing to catch and manhandle the hogs for sticking and bleeding the hogs, putting them in and taking them out of the scalder, scraping off the hair, and hanging up and gutting them. Young kids would always be on hand to look and watch the proceedings, but after the killing and bleeding of the first hog, that would be enough for them and they would flee in horror, especially if it was their first hog-killing.

At many hog-killings there was often some whiskey to drink (bootleg or otherwise). While the water in the scalder was being heated, many would have a drink or two to warm their blood on a frosty morning. When the water was finally hot enough and the men were feeling good from their whiskey, they would go to the pen and a couple of the strongest men would catch and throw a hog down on his back and hold the hog until he had been stuck. When the hog had bled out he was put into the scalder (dead now, of course) until his hair was ready to come off, five minutes, more or less. The hog was then pulled onto a large scraping platform on one side of the scalder and the hair would be scraped off down to the bare hide. Then the hog would be hung up, head down, from a large timber beam that was erected for that purpose, and was called a hog-gallows. At this point, the hog was gutted out, washed out, and the carcass was propped open to dry and cool.

This same procedure followed through to the last hog. A small intestine, called a casing, was separated from the main intestines. These were usually scraped and thoroughly cleaned by the women folk. This casing was later used to stuff sausage. The livers were salvaged out of the innards and hung out to freeze during the frosty night so that fresh liver could be cooked the next day.

After all the hogs had been killed, gutted, and dried out, they were put on the barn floor, where they would also freeze overnight, and the following day would be cut up into various cuts of meat: hams, shoulders, side loins, and chine bone sections. So the foregoing ends the first day of hog killing.

The second day of hog work commences with the men going to the barn where the hogs have lain all night and have become stiff and frosty. The men liked the meat to be frosty and the weather cool, as the meat butchers better and there is no risk of spoilage, as would happen once-in-a-while if the temperature got too high.

The men used butcher knives and axes ground to a keen edge to chop and butcher the meat. The hog heads were chopped off first, then the hog was chopped length-wise down each side of the spine. Next, the hind quarters were cut off and when trimmed became the hams. The same procedure took place with the front quarters which are called the shoulders. The mid-section of each side of the hog was squared up and referred to as a side of meat or side of bacon. The length wise strip containing the spine was cut up into pork chops or pork roasts.

All of the meat trimmings, part of the sides, and part of the head went into a tub and were cut into strips for making sausage. The fatty parts were cut off to cook and make into lard. The best part of the lard fat covered the ribs on each side of the hog; this was called leaf fat and made beautiful white lard after being cooked, cooled, hardened, and put into lard cans. The ribs were trimmed out of the sides and plenty of lean meat was always left to later bake as spare-ribs, which were stuffed and rolled around sage dressing baked in a wood-burning stove oven.

While the men were butchering in the barn, the women folk were cutting the trimming for sausage, and cutting fat into one-inch cubes and cooking it for lard. Also, large skillets were filled with fresh pork liver and pork tenderloins for the noon-day meal and for supper-time and served with mashed potatoes, pork gravy, coleslaw, pickles, and hot biscuits.

By the end of the second day, the hogs had been cut up, the lard made, and the sausage meat ground up. Grinding was done by hand grinders. The men, women, and children had a busy day with all of this activity, but it was just like a big party as some of the neighbors and relatives always joined into help out. So it was hard work, but came with a side of fun, friends, and fellowship.

The third day of hog killing activities were now at hand. Usually the third day just about finished up the hog work for that particular year. After a hearty breakfast of hog liver or fresh sausage along with com- meal hot cakes, plus plenty of hot coffee, work commenced. The meat, as the hams, shoulders, and sides, were be cured by one of two methods: There was the sugar-cure process where the hams, shoulders, and sides are all laid out on a large table or plank benches with the skin sides down, and black molasses was heated to near the boiling point, then poured on very thickly all over the raw meat; then a special kind of salt (coarser than table salt) was patted on thickly over the molasses. The sections of meat were then put into a muslin bag and hung up in the meat house to cure. The molasses and salt mixture would eventually penetrate the meat right to the bone. Along about Easter, one of these sugar-cured hams would be some really fine eating. Some people would also hickory smoke the sugar-cured meats which was a matter of taste.

Another method of curing was the salt brine treatment. A meat barrel was partly filled with water and enough salt to make a brine that was strong enough to float an egg. The hams, shoulders, and sides would be immersed in this brine and kept there for two to three months at which time the salt solution penetrated through the meat to the bone. When taken out of the brine, they would then hang the meat in the smoke-house and smoke slowly over a smoldering fire of either hickory or apple wood. Around Easter, this type of cured meat was also good eating.

These hams would be cooked by just plain boiling as this would draw out the salt. Sometimes after boiling, the women would stick cloves (after removing the skin) into the ham, sprinkle them with pepper, and brown the hams or shoulders a little in the oven. The pig's feet, spare-ribs, and spine sections would be put into the brine the same as the other meats, but were taken out and cooked as needed and were used all through the winter, or until the hams were cured and ready to use.

Meanwhile in the kitchens, the women folk seasoned the fresh sausage and with the use of a hand operated sausage press, stuffed the sausage into the casings. The sausage was seasoned with old-time recipes and instructions, those of which every clan of relatives slightly differed, but were basically the same. Certain quantities of sugar, salt, sage, fresh black and red peppers, and other spices were used in the sausage mixes.

So now, the hog-work was just about finished, except for a few pans of scrapple left to be made. This entailed the boiling of all the cut-off hog skins, livers, and jowls that would then be ground into a pulp, put in deep baking pans and set away for a while to stiffen up so they could then be cut out into slices for frying. Scrapple was very good along with hot cakes.

Before Christmas, the women would make three or four gallons of mince-meat for the holiday and winter pies. The hog-head meat was used to make the mincemeat along with apples, raisins, beef suet, and spices. During the three days of hog-work, and for several days afterward, everybody enjoyed the cooking. Fresh pork liver, pork tenders, and fresh sausage would be fried in big iron skillets, on top of the old-time wood-burning type kitchen ranges. Then a little later on, a piece of the spine section called "chine-bone" meat would be taken out of the brine barrel and baked along with fresh dug yams and rich gravy. Next a rack of spare-ribs would be wrapped around sage dressing and baked. The hog brains were rolled in a flour, pepper, and salt mixture and fried. The pig feet were split, boiled until tender, and then browned down and steamed with vinegar. Chitterlings (a certain intestine) were also cooked and eaten, as was the hog stomach into which sausage and potatoes were stuffed baked.

So, one can say that no part of the hog was wasted. Some of the people even saved the bladders, which would they would let dry; then at Christmastime they would be blown up and tied like balloons, and when jumping on, would explode with a very loud noise heralding the Christmas morn.

This type of hog-butchering activity does not take place anymore in Sassafras Neck, or for that matter, across the nation. If people in the present raise hogs to butcher, they haul them alive to one of the many slaughter houses for butchering and haul the meat back home all wrapped up and ready for the freezer. The good old-time type of hog-killing and butchering shared by the neighbors and relatives all working together and having a good time doing it is another bygone working scene.

Community gathering for "hog killing" event

CHAPTER IX
THE COUNTRY STORE

The country store was always quite a lively business in Sassafras Neck. In my lifetime I can remember three of them located in Warwick, up-neck near the Delaware state line, and in one of them was located local US Post Office. In the neck at the town of Cecilton there were five country stores, a harness shop, two blacksmith shops, a farm machinery and hardware store, and two butcher shops, and of course a local Post Office.

Cecilton was and still is the largest town in Sassafras Neck. In Earleville, the village where I was born and raised, there was one large country store in which the local Post-Office was located. Many of the local Post Offices in those times were located in country stores in many of the towns up and down the Delmarva Peninsula in the rural areas. A mile west of Earleville, on the Pearce Neck Road was a small country store. Three miles south of Earleville at the crossroads of Pond Neck Road and Stemmers Run Road was located another small country store, and this location was called Watts Corner. At

Fredericktown down at the Sassafras River was still another store, with the local Post Office therein. So there were, as one can see, quite a few stores, big and small.

Many, in fact, most of the stores originated in the 1800s and most of them continued in business up until around 1940, but by that time they were in much decline, and some of the smaller ones had closed their doors. In the late 1920's and early 30's, the American and A&P chain grocery stores had located in Middletown, DE; Chesapeake City, MD; and Chestertown, MD, and with people having automobiles and the chain stores having cheaper prices, many of the neck people slowly started to patronize them instead.

The proprietors of the country stores were usually clad in what one might call "slip-on" clothes, woolen or corduroy trousers in winter time, and pants made of lighter weight material in the warmer weather. Most of the time they wore white shirts, but only one a week. Many wore a bow tie and for some reason they most always wore a vest across which a gold chain would hang. Attached to one end would be a gold watch in the lower vest pocket and on the other end a little gold or silver penknife. Many were bald, some were slim and some were stout.

Most of the storekeepers used tobacco in some form. Some smoked cigars, some pipes, a few might chew tobacco, but on account of the women folk coming into the stores quite often, they chewed real neat and kept the brown stains away from the corners of their mouths. The local Post Offices that were in the stores were often managed by the storekeeper's wife or some local lady. Many of the country stores had a second story and most all had a little space somewhere with a roll-top desk which served the proprietor's office, usually with all the pigeon holes jammed with papers and the flat part of the desk cluttered with more papers, pens, pencils, and a bottle or two of ink. A telephone was also fastened to the wall was near the desk.

These stores, in all cases, were equipped with big potbelly stoves that burned mostly the hard anthracite coal and were located near the middle area of the stores on the first floor. Some of these stoves were five or six feet in height and would bum a few tons of coal during the cold winter months. Around the stove, laying on the floor, was usually an iron wagon tire centered around the feet of the stove which was filled with coal ashes for the men to spit tobacco juice into and throw cigar or cigarette butts and match sticks in. As the ashes got filthy, they would have to be cleaned out and refilled with fresh ashes. The storekeeper would pay someone else to do this dirty chore.

All of the country stores were equipped with heavy shutters and a bar of iron would go across the outside and be bolted from the inside the door when the store closed for the night. Even back in those days there were a few thieves around, although there is no comparison to the larger amount of thieving of the present. When robbers or other types of criminals were convicted years ago, they were punished and not coddled or played around with by the lawyers and courts, and many times their first crime was their last one, as the needed and timely punishment straightened them out.

The country stores carried or stocked quite a varied assortment of goods and groceries—work clothes, dry goods, boots, shoes, trappers' and hunters' supplies, hardware and many other items. Let's take a look at the stock and arrangements of one of the larger country stores such as the Earleville one where my family and many relatives did their shopping, or as everyone used to say, "did their dealing."

In the back end of the store building were all of the tobaccos on shelves. Wooden boxes contained various brands of flat square or plug chewing tobacco such as Apple, Brown's Mule, Cyclone, Better than Gold, and Days Work, which sold for ten cents a plug (which was about a three-inch square). Some of the chewing tobaccos were wrapped in heavy paper sacks such as Beech-Nut, Red-Man, Mail-Pouch, and Silver-Cup. These tobaccos in the pouches were in rough shreds.

The store countertop always had a contraption for cutting the plug tobacco. Also there was pipe smoking tobaccos in tin cans, rather small cans designed to be carried in the hip pocket with brand names like Prince-Albert, Tuxedo, Union-Leader; and there were those in paper pouches with names such as Sensation and Granger, and then some sold in little cloth bags that were used for rolling your own cigarettes with names like Dukes Mixture, RJR, and Golden Grain.

Nearby was a large assortment of pipes—corncob, briar, and

cherry wood smoking bowls—and when I was a boy one could buy a little clay pipe with a reed stem for a nickel.

There were boxes of cigars, such as the "44," Red-Dragon, Havana Ribbon and Cinco, which all sold for a nickel a piece. Then there were the Post-Masters, or two-for-a-nickel cigars which came in bright yellow tin cans containing fifty cigars each.

Last but not least was the cigarette, which was at that time just beginning to flourish, but there were only four brands—Chesterfields, Lucky-Strikes, Camels, and Piedmonts. Snuff was also available in little tin cans.

Next we come to the groceries, located toward the rear of the store on shelves that reached the ceiling. The shelves were filled with all kinds of canned goods, bags of flour, corn-meal, salt, Quaker Oats cereal (oatmeal), and Kellogg's Corn Flakes, and in earlier days these were just about the only cereals there were, as no other types of dry cereals had yet been concocted.

The same was true with coffee. The first and only coffee that I can remember was Arbuckle's, which was shipped to merchants in heavy burlap bags in bean form and had to be ground by the store grinder, or at home, since just about every household had a small grinder.

There were many other types of groceries on the shelves. There was always a pickle barrel with the pickles in the brine. Another barrel with salt-mackerel fish was always on hand. A special rack held the various assorted cakes and cookies and fig bars that were sold loose by the pound. Special types of metal bins held all of the different spices, which were also sold loose by the ounce.

A big cake of cheese was also displayed, usually under a screen cover to keep off the flies, which were abundant in the summer time with many people always coming and going in and out of the store. Hanging from the ceiling were Big picnic hams (cured and smoked) wrapped in heavy white waxed paper tied with wide red cord; they each bore a trademarked label, showing a seaman at the wheel of a sailing ship with the brand name Kinghams.

About midway through the store a large glassed-in candy case held many varieties of penny candies. Nearby, another showcase contained harmonicas or mouth organs, hews-harps, everyday watches, and an assortment of pocketknives. This particular showcase fascinated me to no end when I was a boy.

Another section displayed pots, pans, skillets, dishes, and other cookware and tableware. In the front end of the store the dry goods and notions were shelved and displayed.

The shelves held many bolts of dress cloth such as gingham, percale, and muslin sold by the yard. Women customers bought cloth to make housedresses, skirts and blouses, sheets and pillow cases and children's clothes. There were also spools of all kinds of cottons, ribbon materials, and elastics from which garters were made, needles, thimbles, knitting needles, and many sizes and colors of buttons, plus handkerchiefs and men's and women's stockings.

A back room off to one side of the store was referred to as the shoe room with shelves stocked with men's, women's, and children's dress shoes and everyday shoes. Stocked also were gum boots, knee height or high tops, rubber soled cloth upper over shoes called Artics and felt type boots worn inside of over shoes. Most of the rubber footwear bore the trademark of Red Ball-Band or the white arrow by the Hood Rubber Co.; a favorite brand of work shoe was the Chippewa. The upstairs of the store was usually just one big open area filled with stacks of men's everyday work clothes such as overalls, khaki and corduroy trousers, blue chambray shirts for warm weather, flannel shirts for winter weather, work jackets, long-john winter underwear, and BVD one-piece men's summer underwear.

There were also a few items for horse harnesses such as bridles, pads, and collars. One could also find gun shells and steel traps for hunting and trapping. One thing about a country store that was a constant fight to keep under control was the mice and rats because of the storage of food, cheese, cornmeal, flour, meats, and bunches of bananas. The storekeepers had baited traps set everywhere, and every so often when new clerks were broken in their fingers were stung by the mouse traps. Crickets were another problem, as they would come sneaking into the store in the late summer and were destructive to clothes and cloth.

Right after Thanksgiving, the merchants started to get in their shipments of Christmas goodies, and that really did start to put Christmas in your bones. It usually started off with one or two large burlap bags full of fresh coconuts and a few wood buckets of fresh mincemeat being delivered so that the women folk could get started making mince pies and coconut cakes for Christmas. Next to arrive were several wooden buckets of various kinds of Christmas candies, such as sugar candies in pink, green, white, and yellow, hard candy, toy candy, chocolate drops, coconut balls and peanut brittle. Then there were the oranges— sixty years ago Christmas was the only time our Earleville store ever had oranges, as they were not as plentiful as today, and they were full of flavor. I don't think I ever smelled anything so good as the aromas of a country store just before Christmas.

A few times a year the store keepers might go by train to Wilmington, Delaware or by steamboat to Baltimore, Maryland to make personal selections of certain types of merchandise; otherwise various salesmen from the big wholesale houses in the cities would periodically make their visits to the country stores once a month.

These salesmen were mostly referred to as "drummers" (they drummed up business). They were always well dressed in business suits and other appropriate clothing according to the season of the year. They always had a strong odor of cologne about them; they carried large leather satchels, holding their lists of foods, order forms, etc. The ordered goods were shipped by steamboat from Baltimore; or by freight from Wilmington to the Pennsylvania Railroad Station in Middletown, Delaware. Most of the time the merchandise came packed in wooden boxes, crates, and wood barrels. The stronger boxes would eventually be strung out along the outsides of the counters on both sides of the store for people to sit on.

Nighttime activity at the country store was a little bit different than that during the daytime. During the day, the customers would usually come in, make their purchases, and go, as most were busy in the daytime, especially during the spring, summer, and fall with the planting, growing, and harvesting of crops.

In the evenings after supper was over, the folks (mostly men) started to collect in the country stores. Many country stores had a shed type of porch along the front. The Earleville store had this type of porch, which wound from the front around and down the south side of the building.

In the warm weather there were always wooden goods boxes and a couple of empty sugar barrels under the porches for people to sit. The men would sit around smoking, chewing tobacco, and spitting all over creation; some would be talking about the crops, others about cows, horses, and just about anything. One or two might be reading the evening newspapers, *The Baltimore Sun*, the *Evening Bulletin* or the *County Weekly*. Always, someone was getting up to go in the store and reappear with a soft drink, ice cream or fresh cigar.

Once in a while, a couple men would get into an argument over something and a fist fight would occur, and the proprietor would have to tell them to fight out in the road and not on his store property. For the most part though, the people gathered were all friends and neighbors from the west end of Sassafras Neck. Then there was a little clique of black men off to one side, and every now and then one would be called upon to verify some subject or issue being discussed. Some of us young boys would sit nearby listening to some of the elder conversation, or play hide-and-seek or chase-the-fox over in the school yard across the road.

Some of the farmers that lived near Earleville walked into the store in the evening, some came on horseback or in buggies, and a few would drive in their Model-T Fords, little four-cylinder Chevys, or little Overland autos. A few of the financially better off people had Studebakers, Nash's, or Buicks, and I can remember one Oakland.

Occasionally a few women folk would come to the store, and they would always collect at the front in the dry goods and notions area, and near the Post Office which was operated by the store keeper's wife, usually on Saturday afternoons as the women took care of the grocery shopping for the household. If they lived on a farm they would bring market baskets of eggs and homemade butter and trade them off for groceries, as was the custom in the early 1900s. The butter and eggs would sometimes also be bought the minority of village people who did not have a milk cow or did not raise poultry.

When the warm summer weather was over and cool fall evenings came, the men gathered inside the store where the goods boxes were set up. Also, there were nail kegs to sit on, as all country stores sold nails. As the fall nights got longer and colder, the pot belly stove was fired up and the men continued their talk and discussions as usual. The tobacco smoke from pipes, cigars, and cigarettes got so thick one could almost cut it with a knife. Once in a while, a tobacco chewer would not be watching where he was spitting and his spit would land on the hot barrel of the stove, sending up a rancid smelling steam; all the time the din of many voices, laughter, and even shouting filled the store.

All of this was a sight to see and hear. However, it was a way of life and everybody was content and happy for the most part.

The nearby Post Office was managed by the Earleville storekeeper's wife, a spry little lady who in her younger days was a country school teacher. The Post Office was open from 7 a.m. to 7 p.m., and her salary at one time was only eight hundred dollars a year, and she worked a twelve-hour day except for taking time out for dinner and supper. She did have a helper, the rural carrier, to sort out mail.

The Post Office mistress was kept busy. Back in the day many, and indeed, most people would get money orders to send to mail order houses, such as Sears Roebuck, Montgomery Ward, Bella's Hess and Gimbels, to buy things. Money orders then were all made out in longhand with pen and ink.

There used to be just one mail run a day until after the 1920s when there was a morning mail and an evening mail. The Earleville people and others in the west end of Sassafras Neck looked forward to getting the mail and newspapers because, even in the late 20s, they didn't have radios yet. The *Philadelphia Bulletin* and the *Baltimore Sun* back then sold for two cents a copy, two cent stamps would mail a letter, and penny postcards could be had.

The rural mail carrier lived in Earleville and carried the mail every afternoon down into all the west end necks in his Model-T Ford in good weather, and by horse and wagon in bad winter weather, as all the roads were dirt roads and got bad in the winter thaws.

If the evening papers were reporting on a murder trial or any very important news, then that would be the topic of much discussion by the men who frequented the country store. I remember the case of the Lindberg baby kidnapping affair, which gave evening crowds a topic for some time. Even before radio days when there was a big championship boxing match such as heavyweights Dempsey vs. Willard, Firpo vs. Dempsey, Dempsey vs. Tunney or even Benny Leonard, the great lightweight; there would always be a big scramble to get an evening paper to read all about it.

Let us now look into the butcher shop business. The larger one of the two butcher shops located in Cecilton butchered and sold pork, lamb, veal, and beef. The pork, lamb, and veal were the same as everywhere else, but the type of beef was not. The proprietor bought most all of the animals from the local farmers and he had a pasture lot a couple of acres in size in back of his town property where he would keep his acquired animals until he slaughtered them in his slaughter house. The beef was actually the meat of the milk cow that the farmers would let go, mostly on account of its age or because he had an over-stocked herd; but when fattened, believe it or not it made very good tasting beef, even it if was a little tough now and then. A section of shin bone made the most wonderful pot of beef and vegetable soup.

One proprietor made excellent scrapple and sausage. Veal was from mostly the bull calves. The butcher shops did most of their business on Saturdays and especially on Saturday night. The general stores at that time did not handle any fresh meats, but later on a few of them did once they installed large refrigerators that used blocks of ice.

The leading butcher in Cecilton, Mr. Griffith, had a hired man—black, short, and chunky—whom everyone called "Stump." On Saturday mornings, Stump would load the Model T Ford butcher wagon with an assortment of meats and would come to Earleville to serve the village folk. He would always have on a white apron and wore straw cuffs halfway to his elbows. He would always give a little "down weight," but rarely ever charged for it, as he was a very good hearted man. He weighed the meat on the old time hanging scale.

During the summer runs no ice was used and back in those days I don't remember anyone in Earleville that had an icebox. Once the meat purchase was made the meat was very quickly put into a pot and cooked, or put in a bucket attached to a long rope and was hung way down inside the deep bricked up wells where it was damp and very cool, where it would keep in most cases until the next day.

Everyone had a well platform over the well on which hung a rope box that was used as an access to the well if repairs were needed, which was often the case. Butter, milk, dressed poultry, and other perishable goods were also temporarily stored on the end of a rope down in the well. This was, I guess, a risky way to handle perishable goods by modern standards. However, I don't remember a single case of food poisoning. If the perishables didn't look or smell as they should, they were not used. (Imagine what the Board of Health would have to say today about such goings-on.)

All in all, the country stores and shops played a big part in the everyday life of the people of Sassafras Neck. They were entertainment and conversation, fellowship, news centers, argument centers, tobacco juice and tobacco smoke centers, as well as merchandise centers. The old type country stores and shops are now all past history in the contemporary times in which we live, but for those of us who are old enough to have experienced the old time way of Sassafras Neck, they provided many fond memories.

H. S. Duhamell

DEALER IN

General Merchandise

...

EARLEVILLE, MD.

J. E. FERGUSON
Successor to Wm. H. Brown
BAKER AND CONFECTIONER
A new line of Fine Confectionery, Fancy Crackers and Cakes
Phone 32   CECILTON, MARYLAND

JAMES SMITH
GENERAL MERCHANDISE
Dry Goods, Notions, Groceries
CECILTON, MARYLAND

JOHN H. BLACK   CECILTON, MD.
Drugs, Chemicals, Patent Medicines
Perfumery, Combs, Brushes, Fine Toilet Soaps, Shoulder Braces, Trusses, Supporters, Books and Stationery, Glass, Putty, Paints, Oils, Varnishes, Dye-Stuffs, etc.
Goods selected with care and warranted as represented.

Merchant ad for Cecilton/Earleville in Cecil County Paper

Fashion ad in 1910 Cecil County Newspaper

CHAPTER X
HOME AND FAMILY LIFE IN SASSAFRAS NECK

Home life in the country in Sassafras Neck up until the late 1920s was very different from what it is now in contemporary times.

Most of the farmhouses were fine ones with seven to ten, and sometimes as many as twelve rooms. The houses in Earleville, Cecilton, Warwick, and Fredericktown usually had six to eight rooms on average, and most of the houses had attics with a couple of rooms or just one big open space. The farm tenant houses were much smaller, with three to five rooms.

Most of the homes were adequately but plainly furnished. All were heated by stoves that burned wood or hard coal. Just about all the kitchens were equipped with a large wood burning kitchen range. Usually, in the wintertime, the dining rooms became "sitting rooms" and were heated with either a large wood burning stove or a large type of coal burning stove. The parlors, where the best furniture was kept, were only used on special occasions, like when company came, or the local preacher and his wife would visit, and at Christmas time.

The upstairs rooms were not, as a general rule, heated unless a member of the family was going through a lengthy illness. Almost every bed was equipped with a large sack made of heavy, stripped cloth called ticking, which was stuffed with goose or duck feathers. One could sink down into these feather sacks and cover up with heavy homemade quilts and wool blankets and keep snug and warm during the cold winter nights. So all in all, the people lived plain but were warm, dry, and comfortable, and for the most part content.

Back in the earlier days, families were real close to one another, with the children being close to their parents. In many cases, the grandparents lived in the same house as the children and grandchildren, and sometimes an aunt or uncle would be present. In those days, most people took care of their elders (except in extreme cases) right in their homes and they were not put in nursing homes as many are today. The admiration and respect for each member of the family was very prevalent in bygone days. Even when old people happened to go blind or became paralyzed or crippled, they were kept at home among their old friends and their own folks until they passed away.

Every mealtime—breakfast, dinner or supper—was a great time. There was no electric power back then in the neck towns and villages, so in the winter, coal oil lamps were used for lighting and supper was cooked and eaten in the lamplight. All three meals for the day were hearty ones. There was no such thing as "lunch" in the middle of the day. In fact, the noon meal was the biggest meal. People in those days worked harder and expended much more energy than modern people of today.

Breakfast, of course, started off the day and usually consisted of cornmeal hotcakes with sausage, scrapple, or bacon, eggs, a skillet full of home fried potatoes, and sometimes ham and eggs fried in the ham grease for flavor. For dinner there were many varied foods— boiled ham or pork shoulder with cabbage and turnips or wild greens, as they came in season; baked chicken, duck, or goose; baked fish, such as shad or rockfish; chicken, beef, pork, squirrel, or rabbit potpie, plus many types of stews; beef and vegetable and bean soups, and in winter always a pot of hominy. Supper was mostly the leftovers from dinner of which there was always plenty. However, if the leftovers were not enough they were supplemented with a big egg omelet, platter of fried ham or fried salt herring, vegetables, blackberry or strawberry shortcake, jellies, preserves, black molasses, homemade bread and biscuits, and plenty of coffee and milk to drink. Of course, the items of food served depended somewhat on the seasons of the year.

Country folk in Earleville and the west end of Sassafras Neck, even in the first quarter of the century, did not believe in working on the Sabbath Day and, if so, only did what was absolutely necessary. As a result, the women folk cooked and baked on Saturdays for Sunday dinner and supper.

People for the most part were God-fearing and adhered to the Ten Commandments and other Bible teachings. Even some people who did not attend church very often believed in and feared God, and by the same token, some people who attended church regularly would still swear and curse some through the week.

Sunday afternoons were usually filled with visits to friends, neighbors and relatives who might live in Earleville or across the creeks. My mother played the piano and my father played a little on the violin and loved to sing, as he had a good tenor voice. So many times when we had visitors they usually had a singing session. I remember some of the old songs they used to sing like the World War I tunes, "Keep the Home Fires Burning," "Parlez Vous," "Little Nest in the West," and "Beautiful Ohio," and other older ones like "My Old Kentucky Home," and "Darling Nellie Gray." They would invariably wind up with "Old Virginia State Where I Was Born," or "There Is a Long Trail a Winding."

Children were taught to respect their elders, to be honest, not to lie, and how to work and do things. Children also got punished if they were caught lying, or being dishonest, or disrespectful, and as a result most of the time when they grew to be teenagers they did not run wild as so many do in modem times. The ones that became unmanageable wound up in a reform school, but this was rare.

As small boys, my brother and I, along with Mom, used to gather nuts from the woods and fields, such as black walnuts, hickory nuts, chestnuts, and just a few hazel nuts, and the nuts would be used in winter for cakes, candies, and homemade black walnut taffy. Also, in the summertime we picked lots of wild blackberries, and hunted for wild greens.

Many people had porch swings and rocking chairs on their porches and in the long summer evenings would sit outside and watch the moon come up or go down, the stars as one would fall now and then, and the fireflies, or lightening bugs as we used to call them. Night birds could be heard, such as the whip-poor-will, the nigh-hawk, and the tink-tanks and bullfrogs in the marshes and creeks.

At home in the wintertime after supper, lessons for school had to be studied, but then there was popcorn to pop, taffy candy to make, or occasionally a pan full of homemade fudge candy. Near bedtime mothers would read bedtime stories to the small children. Edgar Rice Burroughs was a favorite; he wrote stories for children about the woodlands, and ponds, and his characters were small wild animals such as Tillie the Turtle, Sammy Skunk, Jonnie Muskrat, and Danny Beaver, to name a few. There also was the old time Mother Goose picture story and rhyme book. One of my big favorite stories in ·this book was "Who Killed Cock-Robin." The older children would usually sit around the kitchen table after supper in winter, studying lessons by lamplight.

Most of the housewives had a regular routine for housework, like washing on Monday, ironing on Tuesday, patching and mending on Wednesday, a bit of everything on Thursday, cleaning on Friday, baking on Saturday, and Church on Sunday.

Many women, and some men, were never so busy that they could not take a short nap after the noon meal. My own mother always managed to take about an hour nap during the middle of the afternoon and still does. If one lived on a farm, a great thing to do on a rainy day would be to go to the horse stable loft and go to sleep for a while on the hay.

Hardly anyone in Sassafras Neck worked on Sunday, except to feed the cattle, horses and poultry, and to milk the cows. Most of the farm people never worked on Sunday afternoons, and since all of the equipment up until the 1920s was horse drawn, gave their animals a day of rest as well. In contrast, today it seems that with all of the mechanical equipment and big diesel tractors, one can see many farmers plowing, planting, and harvesting on Sunday as if it were just another day in the week.

People are bound to get sick once in a while, so let's take a look at some of the illnesses that occurred in the early part of the present century that plagued the people of Sassafras Neck. First on the list was the common cold, of which many of the Neck people sooner or later had and, of course, still exists today. The difference, however, of then and now is that many years ago people did not pay as much attention to colds as they do today. This is not to say that ignoring a cold was good. The old timers seldom stopped work, which in most cases, was outdoors; they just kept on going. But in a few cases now and then, neglect pushed a person into pneumonia. Neglect, I think, was due in part to the scarcity of doctors, clinics, and hospitals.

The mothers did use many home remedies on the children and on the grownups for colds. The most often used was the mustard plaster; a mixture of dry mustard made into a paste and smeared on a piece of muslin cloth which was overlaid with another piece of muslin and then laid on the chest for a short time to break up congestion.

When I was a child, my mother had, on many a cold night, got out of her bed to heat a teaspoon full of Vaseline over a lighted lamp chimney to melt it, sprinkled on a little sugar, and gave it to us to ease coughing. Another cough medicine she gave us was a scant teaspoon of sugar with a few drops of coal oil. Much hot lemonade was made and sipped before going to bed. (Men would sometimes use a little whiskey in the hot lemonade.)

Whooping cough was a dreaded thing in children some years ago. Two home remedies for this would often be used. One was a "sheep pill" tea consisting of little round balls of sheep manure brewed just like tea. Another was to milk a female horse, heat the milk and sip it. More than a few children died of whooping cough in the older days.

But even though people sometimes didn't pay enough attention to coughs and colds and sometimes died of pneumonia, people of fifty or more years ago seemed to be physically tougher and more enduring than people of today. They had to be to work and go and do like they had to in the country in Sassafras Neck, and most anywhere else in the country back then.

There were many cases of measles, mumps, chicken pox, and scarlet fever, mostly confined to children. Children and adults also suffered a lot though with earaches and toothaches. As a boy, I remember my father gearing up a two-horse carriage team in late winter and driving from almost the end of Pearce Neck clear up to the town of Elkton—a distance of twenty or more miles—to get some teeth pulled. He left early and it was dark when he got back. That was the only town near us that had a dentist. Later on, when I was about seven years old, a general practitioner doctor came to practice in Cecilton and would pull teeth in an emergency, and pulled the first two jaw teeth I ever had pulled. Most every household kept a small bottle of sweet-oil for toothaches.

Diabetes and Diphtheria were dreaded diseases since there was no cure for them. Some people died with tuberculosis, as it was also an incurable disease. My own father died of it at thirty-four years of age. At the time I was nine, my brother was eight, and my mother was twenty-eight.

It is wonderful that most of the old time incurable diseases are now curable today. However, the people of the Neck fifty or more years ago rarely died of cancer or heart trouble.

Enough of illness and diseases, let's move on to the more pleasant subject of the holidays. Once Thanksgiving had passed, the harvest season was over and the hog work was done, it was time to get ready for Christmas.

Preparations would start off in the morning around the first of December with women folk chopping up candied fruits, citron rind, lemon peel, prunes, and raisins. Following this, a stiff cake batter would be made up with various spices for flavoring. Then after the noon meal, the cut-up fruit would be mixed in with the cake batter, the kitchen range would be fired up to the right heat for the big oven, and the cakes would be baked in dishpans. When they were done they weighed from eight to twelve pounds each, and if the pans were real big they weighed up to fifteen pounds. When they were baking they really did smell good with all of the different spices that were mixed in the cake batter.

My grandmother, mother, and aunt all worked together every year on this. While baking, the women would push a broom straw down through the cake to test to see if and when the cake was fully baked. When the big cakes were done, they were wrapped up in a special cloth, and when the cake cooled they would brush either wine or grape juice all over the cake which would give it even another added flavor blend.

Hardly any of the remaining neck people make these fruit cakes anymore. However, my wife and my elderly mother and a few of the older folks still make them, but only small ones weighing about three to four pounds each. One big reason for the decline of the big fruitcake was the outmoding of the old time big wood or coal burning kitchen ranges with the big cast iron ovens. They were wonderful ovens to bake in.

At about this time of the year (nearing Christmastime) people would be rushing to send money orders to Sears Roebuck, Montgomery Ward, and other mail order houses for Christmas toys, clothes, and presents. The country stores in Earleville and Cecilton would stock quite a few toys, such as little wagons, tricycles, tin horns, doll babies, and little BB guns (only single shot in those earlier days), cap pistols, and pop guns.

With Christmas getting closer, the next baking affair would be the making of the layer cakes. Mom always made two—one a coconut cake made with coconut milk and fresh coconut grated up and put all around the outside of the cake on the white icing, and the second a black walnut cake with the cracked nut meat chopped up into the cake batter. After the cake was baked and iced, the large kernels of the walnuts would be stuck into the icing atop the cake for decoration. Once in a while Mom would switch to a hickory nut cake instead of the black walnut cake. These two baked and completed layer cakes would be put into lard cans and set away in the hallway to keep fresh until Christmas.

The next item was a big batch of chocolate fudge candy, with black walnut meat mixed in the candy. When this was cooked, cooled, and cut into one inch squares, it was placed into metal cans to keep fresh until Christmas.

By this time, Christmas would be only ten or so days away and the mail order packages would start arriving at the local Post Office. Children would start getting curious while mothers tried to keep the packages hidden until Christmas Eve, at which time, of course, Santa would come down the chimney and find the toys and presents and put them under the Christmas Tree.

When we were only two or three days away from Christmas Day, a little more baking still had to be done. Most of the Sassafras Neck people always had to have a batch of Maryland "beat biscuits" to go with the Christmas dinner. A big bundle of dough would be made using the fresh hog lard, then it would be laid out on a stout wooden bench or biscuit block and pounded with the blunt end of an axe, rolled up and then pounded again and again about eighteen times, which took at least a half hour. After this was finished the women would tear off small pieces of dough and form them into small round biscuits the size of a golf ball which would be baked until brown on top. Following the biscuit baking, the next and last thing was to make and bake a mince pie and a pumpkin pie for Christmas Dinner dessert and then all the baking would be finished.

During the week before Christmas, chicken salad was made and stored. Some of the neck folks had two or three large Muscovy ducks dressed and ready for the oven, although some preferred goose or baked chicken. In later years many people had started to raise turkeys, and they soon became a favorite for the Christmas dinner. Most everyone would also bake a ham to have through the holidays.

Once the food was ready, it was time to get the Christmas tree. Most people went to the woods to get the tree on Christmas Eve. Cedar trees in years gone by were numerous in the Neck and that was the standard for most everyone. The village people or anyone who did not have a woods could always to go their farmer friends or neighbors and get a tree; there was never a charge, they just asked permission. So the fresh tree with the cedar smell was brought in and set up in the dining room or parlor to later be trimmed by Santa Clause.

Finally, Christmas Day arrived. Santa had come and gone and the family had been up since early in the morning opening presents, the children playing with their toys. The dinner table was set and dinner was ready—baked poultry, dressing, gravy, sliced ham, mashed potatoes, sweet potatoes, homemade pickles, jelly, chicken salad, and Maryland beat biscuits, with mince and pumpkin pies for dessert. Later on in the day there was fruitcake, pie, chocolate or coconut cake, and maybe a little homemade wine to go with the cake. So ended Christmas Day, but actually the good spirits and food lingered all week into the New Year's holiday.

After New Year's Day, thoughts began to turn away from

Christmas toward other interests and pastimes. Usually the snow season was upon us and the young people would turn to sledding, sleighing, and skating in the evenings.

Financially speaking, the home and family life I've described was more or less typical of the average family under moderate circumstances, although the financial and material status of west end Sassafras Neck families was quite varied.

Some families were considered well off if they owned and operated big farms or other types of businesses. Others who owned small farms were of medium income, some were below average, and several were barely making it, Then again, some families had a lot of "get up and go," and a few were "come day, go day, God send Sunday" type of people. However, most anyone at all could eat well if he desired, because people in bygone years raised just about all their food so very little cash had to be spent for it.

In these times the home and family were very important. Most parents were proud of their children and loved them, and the children looked up to their parents with respect. Family reunions were very prevalent fifty or more years ago, whereas today they seem to be rare.

Families in recent times seem to have broken down, and this is not a good trend. This nation of ours (The United States of America) was founded, raised up, and sustained in great part by families, and I believe that if they fall apart, as they apparently seem to be doing currently, our great freedom-based nation could crumble and fall. I hope this will never happen, but it does bear some serious thought.

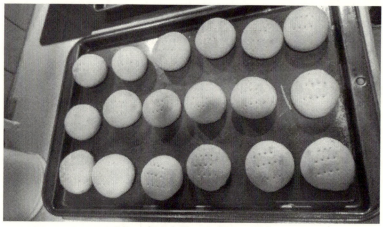
Maryland "beat biscuits"

Maryland Beat Biscuit Recipe

1. 7 cups all-purpose unbleached flour
2. 1 teaspoon salt
3. 1 cup of lard (not vegetable shortening)
4. 2 cups cold water added as needed to form dough ball (less is better)
5. Optional: some use a pinch of sugar and/or baking powder.
6. Sift all dry ingredients in a large bowl; Slowly work in small pieces of lard (fingers work well) & slowly add cold water until you have a stiff dough ball. Once stiff ball is formed it's time to find a work area or sturdy table sprinkled lightly with flour to begin beating with heavy hammer or blunt end of a heavy axe. Beat and roll back up into a ball repeatedly until the dough starts to bubble or blister (pop), usually 30+ minutes of beating. Pull dough and form golf ball-size biscuits, place on baking pan, flatten slightly & use a fork to prick the centers.
7. Preheat oven to 475° to 480° F and bake for approx. 15-20 minutes or until slightly brown on top, depending on individual ovens. Makes 3 to 4 dozen biscuits. Enjoy.

CHAPTER XI
EDUCATION IN SASSAFRAS NECK

In the west end of Sassafras Neck there were the following grade schools that served first through seventh grades: Earleville School No. 9; Ponds and Grove Neck School called "Stumptown;" Pearce Neck School No.7; and Veazey's Neck School referred to as the "Fingerboard School." There was also a small school between Pearce Neck and Ponds Neck on Stemmers Run Road for black children a grade school in Fredericktown, overlooking the Sassafras River.

   The grade schools were wood frame, clapboard, one-room affairs for all seven classes or grades. Up neck was the Wards Hill Road School, the Warwick School, and the Middle Neck School. The grade schools were all on par with one another regarding size, number of pupils, and the fact that each had one woman teaching each school, but since I went to Earleville School, I will use this as a typical example in describing the grade schools in Sassafras Neck.

They all had a fair sized schoolyard; some were fenced around with a white-washed wood fence. Most all of the school buildings, on the front, had an entrance vestibule which contained a coat rack, stoneware water cooler, shelves on which to set lunch boxes, and another shelf type bench to hold a water basin and soap cup. A flag pole thirty feet high made of cedar wood stood near the front of the school building. In the rear of the school yard were outdoor toilets—one for the boys and one for the girls— with wood shields in front of each one. Also nearby there was another small building called the coal house, in which hard coal was stored to burn in the schoolhouse stove in cold weather.

In the rear of the inside of the school was a long black board of slate the width of the room and a raised platform on which the teacher's desk sat. In the front end of the room was a big potbelly iron stove which furnished heat, with a large iron tea kettle sitting on top for hot water when needed.

There were six rows of school desks (two students sat at each desk), all facing the blackboard and the teacher's desk. There was also a big cupboard in the front of the room which held the school books and one great big encyclopedia book.

A small Victrola sat on a stand near the teacher's desk and an American flag stood nearby. There were only three records for the Victrola—"Maryland My Maryland," "The Star Spangled Banner," and "My Country Tis of Thee." US patriotism was stressed in the country schools when I was a schoolboy.

The teacher's desk contained many textbooks. The top of the desk could also be raised, and inside were many other smaller items, including a few personal things belonging to the teacher. A large bell with a handle was kept on top of the desk and was used to call the pupils to order at morning, mid-morning, noon, and mid-afternoon recesses. The teacher would reach out of a window to ring the bell in order to make sure the children would hear it.

Going into the vestibule, there was always (especially in warm weather) a very rank, rancid smell due to the various types of lunch foods in the lunch boxes and bags. The odor was a mixture of hard-boiled eggs, sandwiches made up with strong country butter, longhorn cheese, raw onions and country ham, plus an Ivory Soap smell from kids washing their hands.

Earleville School, from year to year, had fifty to sixty pupils for all seven grades. There was no such thing as a kindergarten in Sassafras Neck in the early 1900s. Children started attending school at about age six and were anywhere from twelve to fourteen years of age when they finished the seven grade, depending on individual intelligence. The first three grades were spent learning reading, ABCs, spelling, and counting, and from then on reading, writing, arithmetic, spelling, history, and grammar.

My school teacher at the Earleville country school was a tall, well built, motherly type of woman and was never married. In fact, in the earlier days most of the women teachers rarely married. My own teacher lived right in Earleville with her widowed father. The pupils and just about everyone else called her "Miss Olive". She taught at Earleville school for many years and I do believe she enjoyed her career very much. She seemed to have a personal interest in every pupil and was well-liked by all the down neck country folks.

Miss Olive Oldham was unquestionably the boss of the school and was a strict disciplinarian, knowing how to correct and discipline. Indeed, once in a while she would lay on the paddle in extreme cases.

She also had to perform first aid to the pupils. Almost daily some kid would cut a finger, get bruised, get something stuck in his eye, or get sick to his stomach. She would bind up their wounds after using peroxide and iodine, or give a dose of essence of peppermint to ease the stomach. Many times over the years, if a child came to school with a dirty face, hands, or ears she would take him or her to the vestibule and scrub the child with a wash rag, or sometimes in extreme cases, with a brush, and of course, Ivory Soap. Many kids in those days had large boils (something one does not see too often in these later years). Sometimes while playing in the schoolyard a boil would burst and this would require considerable first aid. Miss Olive would get the tea kettle down off the potbelly stove, bathe the affected area with hot water, apply a special salve, and bind it up. Most times, the child would go back out in the yard and continue playing.

Even kids back in those days were much tougher physically than those today. I remember one time there was an outbreak of the "itch," which, of course, was contagious, and many of us pupils had to go the local country doctor to get prescription medicine and salves for this condition. Miss Olive also kept a sharp lookout for signs of head lice. If she suspected any certain child or family of children, she would take them to the school vestibule and roughly examine them. If nits or lice were found they would be sent home. When they returned after the condition had supposedly cleared up, Miss Olive would thoroughly re-examine them to make sure they were free of lice. Many times in winter Miss Olive would, without any advance notice, order all the windows in the school room to be opened to let in fresh air, and we would go through a deep breathing exercise for about five minutes.

All in all, the women teachers in country schools in the earlier 1900s were a much different, tougher breed than present day teachers. There were exceptions, but when one finished seven years of grade school in Earleville he could read any kind of literature, spell most ordinary words, be familiar with the geography and history of his country (USA), write a proper letter, add, multiply, and divide in regard to arithmetic, and do fractions, decimals and square roots. I have to say that some of today's high school graduates cannot match the old country schools' seven grades of education when it comes to the quality of education they received. In this day and age, it is hard to believe how one woman in a one room country school could teach fifty to sixty pupils in seven grades for a nine-month school year, year after year, with no modern amenities such as hot and cold running water, electricity, and modern toilet plumbing—but they did and were absolutely dedicated to their teaching careers and to the children.

On a typical country school day, the routine went something like this: most children would be on the school grounds by 8 a.m. and play until school was called to order at 9 a.m. Miss Olive would appear a little before the bell rang and the pupils streamed into school and took their respective seats at their desks. Then all would salute the American Flag and say the Pledge of Allegiance, which was followed by the Lord's Prayer. After this, the various grades of arithmetic classes would begin one after another.

In the morning, there would also be history and geography classes. There was a mid-morning recess of about fifteen minutes. At twelve noon there was an hour's lunch period and playtime. The Earleville kids mostly went home for lunch unless there was exceptionally bad weather. The farm boys and girls, of course, always brought their lunches.

At 1 p.m. school was called back in session. In the afternoon, reading, writing, spelling, and grammar classes here held. There was also a mid-afternoon recess of fifteen minutes. School would let out at 4 p.m. During these recess and noon hour periods, the kids played various games like hide-and-seek, run across, Anthony-over, and chase the fox. In the winter (Earleville school was fortunate to have a nice sized pond in one corner), the children went sliding and sledding on the frozen pond.

The boys wrestled a lot and sometime a wrestling match would end up in a fist fight. Boys in the sixth and seventh grades were beginning to notice girls and would pick out their little girl friends, then rivalries occurred and also brought about fist fights. Talk of these fights rarely got back to the teacher, unless a bloody nose wouldn't stop bleeding. Then, Miss Olive would find out who was involved and the fighters and punish them by making them stay inside for a few days and not allowing them to participate in playtime.

Many times at the start of the New Year, tenant farmers would move to another farm, and once in a while a farm family from over the river in Kent County would move into Sassafras Neck and there would be news of a strange girl starting school, which would stir the boys up and also usually cause fisticuffs.

In the cold weather, Miss Olive would designate a couple of boys to fill up the coal buckets and carry them in so that she could stoke the fire in the potbelly stove to keep the heat going all night.

During the school year, students looked forward to several special events. On the first of November the school always had a fall festival which was held to raise a little money to buy a few things for the children's benefit such as games to entertain students on bad weather days when they couldn't go outside to play—games like carom boards, checkers, dominoes and Parcheesi.

In the weeks leading up to the festival, pupils would be asked to inquire if their mothers would make either a cake or homemade candy. Miss Olive would make the lemonade. The ice cream was ordered from a man and his son who had an ice cream parlor in Cecilton. The son, "Dixie" as everyone called him, would deliver the ice cream in the late afternoon—five gallons each of chocolate and vanilla in metal cans packed all around with cracked ice in big wooden tubs.

The school would reopen after suppertime to receive the donations of cakes and candies, which would be arranged on makeshift tables up near the blackboard for slicing and serving. Miss Olive was a good teacher and well-liked by all the parents and a result, the donations flocked in. There would be chocolate, coconut, lemon, sponge, and devil's food cakes; chocolate fudge, divinity fudge, and cream candies; and also the lemonade and ice cream would be on hand.

Many Sassafras Neck people attended these annual fall festivals, as they liked to eat the festival food and also they were interested in the school and their children. The festivities started at about 7:30 p.m. and the folks would sit and eat ice cream, cake, and candy, drink lemonade, and talk and chat the evening away, and a good time was had by all. Even the country store profited from this festival as it brought more business from the festival crowd.

Another time the pupils looked forward to was the last day of school before it closed for the Christmas and New Year's holidays. The school provided a Christmas treat and there were no classes in the afternoon. Prior to this day we exchanged names and everyone would bring in a wrapped gift for the student whose names they drew.

In the morning, "Dixie Cup" ice cream would be delivered packed in ice, as well as cakes donated by the parents for the afternoon treats. A little cedar tree would also be brought in by some of the larger boys and the girls would trim it and lay all the gifts nearby.

When the afternoon arrived Miss Olive would start the party off by telling or reading a special Christmas story. This was followed by the exchange of gifts and then ice cream and cake. It was a joyful time; everyone would have their fill and then we would all start to depart for home, happy not to have to attend school until after the holidays and full of anticipation for Christmas.

Snowstorms and bad weather in January and February made it hard for the neck children to get to school, and as a result, attendance was down during these first two months of the year. However, March soon came along and the twenty-fifth day of March had long since been designated as Maryland Day in recognition of the settling of the state on March 25, 1634. On this special day, we pupils would always wear two little pieces of ribbon on our lapels or collars, one black and the other orange, as these were the colors of the state bird, the Baltimore Oriole. On this morning, the Victrola phonograph would play the record "Maryland My Maryland," the state song, which we would all sing. Early in our grade schooling we would be required to memorize this song. We also memorized "My Country Tis of Thee" and "The Star Spangled Banner." (People in general used to be more patriotic than they are in modern times.)

In the fall and again in the spring, the Cecil County school superintendent would pay the Sassafras Neck schools a visit to see how the schools were coming along. Just about every time the superintendent came, he would arrange to have a large camera supported on a tripod to have pictures taken of the pupils in class and at their desks.

In those days, cameramen had to throw a large black cloth cape over their heads, arms and shoulders and part of the camera, and when they snapped the picture there was a loud report like a shot gun would make, and much blue smoke would ensue. By the time the cameraman was done, all the window sashes had to be raised to let out the smoke. Some little tots who had just started school and had never experienced this would get frightened and cry, and had to be quieted down by Miss Olive. By the end of the school year the children looked forward to Rally Day which fell near the end of May. Rally Day was an all-county affair throughout the State of Maryland and was held in all of the county seats, which for Cecil County was the town of Elkton. These meets were supervised by the Maryland Playground Athletic League. Mostly the high schools in the county competed for championships in baseball, soccer, volleyball, jumping, running, and dodge ball. The winners of the county meets later had a state meet in Baltimore for the state championships.

However, the one big attraction was the Rally Day parade, as all the county grade schools took part in this, displaying their school colors on floats decorated with crepe paper and banners. This used to be a large and colorful parade, and much of the crowds were made up of school parents. This was the only time that we Sassafras Neck children got to go to Elkton. The meet would draw many adult spectators to watch the various competitive games. There were many soda pop and hotdog stands, balloons for sale, and the whole event was much like a fair.

Shortly after the Rally Day event, school examinations were taken to see if the pupils were ready to be passed on to the next grade, and then school ended for the year and the seventh graders moved on to High School (for those who wanted to go—many boys did not, choosing to work on the farm instead or as carpenters, fishermen and trappers.

In Cecilton there was one high school to serve all of Sassafras Neck as well as a separate school building for the Negro children. It was originally a wood frame building with four rooms, one for each of the four years of high school, before it was later remodeled into a dwelling house. My mother was a pupil for a while in this little high school until a larger one was built in the early 1900s, a new brick masonry combination high school and grade school that was constructed in Cecilton called the George Biddle High School or GBHS for short, and she was in the first graduating class

This writer attended this school from 1924 to1928. When I attended, all of the high school and grade school teachers were women with the exception of one male teacher in high school, and while I was still attending he left and was replaced by a woman teacher. I had the same high school principal that my mother had, a middle-aged and well-educated woman named Mary Emily Clark. She was one of the county's first woman principals and could speak and teach in three different languages—Latin, French, and German—and taught history and social science.

I travelled with another boy from Earleville the three miles to Cecilton by horse and carriage for most of the four years we attended high school. His grandmother lived in Cecilton and on her property at that time was a small stable and carriage house near the school. We would unhitch the horse upon arriving in the morning and put him in the stable and the carriage in the adjoining shed. After school we would gear the horse up to the carriage to go home. At the time I was in high school, most of the pupils from out of town were brought to school their parents or older brothers and sisters in horse drawn vehicles or Model-T Fords, Chevy's, or Overland's, which were all four-cylinder cars. Students did not have automobiles to come to school as they do now.

During the four years of high school attendance, a pupil would be taught algebra, physics, geometry, English, advanced history, and a language of one's choice. Our class chose French. Also in high school, there were sports such as soccer in the fall and baseball in the spring for the boys, and volleyball in both fall and spring for the girls. We would compete with other high schools within the county such as Chesapeake City, Elkton, Kenmore, North East, and Perryville as well as at the annual Rally Day athletic meet near the end of the school year.

Nearing the end of the four years, all of the Seniors looked forward to the graduation exercises which consisted of two evenings—Class Night and the following night, which entailed commencement exercises and the presentation of the diplomas. When my mother was going to high school, these exercises were held in the Zion Methodist Church in Cecilton. When this writer graduated, they were held in the later constructed community hall adjoining the Zion Methodist Church.

After four years of high school and graduation, we all went our separate ways. Some of the girls would soon marry, some of the class went to college (but very few because even in those day college was an expensive proposition) and some of the boys joined the Navy, Army, Marines, or Coast Guard. Some would continue on the farms with their parents and some would just get a job. In those days (late 1920s), it was thought that if one's child graduated from high school, he or she had received a fairly good education.

I think it was a good time to have lived as opposed to today's greedy, grabby, go-go world. In my high school days, we boys would sneak a cigarette or pipe to have a smoke. Now high school students, and even some grade school students are causing their parents, teachers, and others much grief and concern over the excessive use of booze and various forms of drugs. Cigarette smoking is now the norm for many pupils, both boys and girls. People have used the saying "old time religion" in referring to those days, but I say we would do well to have some "old time education," laced with common sense added back into our culture today.

Not too many years after I graduated from the George Biddle High School, a new and larger combination high school and grade school was constructed in the west end of Cecilton. After the new construction began the old high school was sold and turned into a movie theater, then resold again and today serves as a hardware store and farm machinery headquarters.

The west end school became a grade school only. In the 1950s a new elaborate high school was constructed in Bohemia Manor just south of Chesapeake City, thus combining the Chesapeake City and Cecilton high schools. In recent years, much taxpayers' money has been spent to usher in what is called "higher education." It may be called that, but in many ways some of us "old time folks" don't think it's any better.

For one thing, the old time discipline and respect is lacking. Of course, this modern world presents more problems than when I was young fifty or more years ago. As far as discipline goes, it is lacking in many families right in the home, and when there is a lack of discipline in the home, children lack respect for their parents, everything, everybody, and even GOD HIMSELF, which eventually will break down a nation.

At the present (1980s) as far as Sassafras Neck is concerned, there have not been any big uproars concerning black and white school integration or busing problems, as has been the case in many parts of the nation (mostly in big cities). It seems to me that some years ago, when black and white integration started to take off, the simplest way to minimize integrated school problems would have been to keep the black schools just as they were, but give blacks the privilege of going to white schools if they chose to do so. In having that choice, I bet most of them would have stayed in their own schools. In my travels up and down the East Coast area I have seen some pretty swanky black schools. It certainly would not have cost the taxpayers more money than is now being spent on extra busing, extra schools and shifting pupils all out of bounds, and would have certainly saved a lot of contention and lawsuits.

It does seem that the modern trend is to deliberately complicate not only education and schooling, but just about everything else, which I would argue is not a good thing.

The way country grade schools and high schools in Sassafras Neck were operated and managed—with good teachers, and pupils who later became good wives, husbands, parents, farmers, businessmen, doctors, engineers, lawyers, churchmen and preachers, watermen, and fishermen—makes me realize I cannot adhere to the arguments of the 1980s that purport today's schools are turning out better students. I suppose you could say today's pupils may be better educated, but to a point that intense education brings with it the sacrifice of their common sense.

Of course, like anywhere else, there were a few "lemons" or bad kids who came in and out of the schools, but by and large the pupils of earlier times turned out to be, for the most part, good, respectable, honest, solid citizens of Sassafras Neck, and of course, other necks and other areas of the country.

George Biddle High School in Cecilton

Cecilton Grammar School, 1908

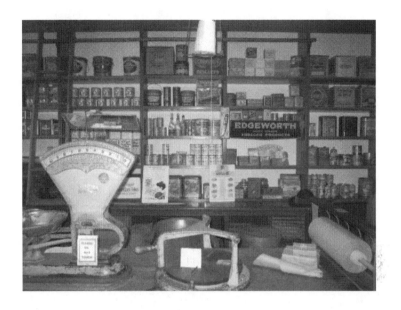

CHAPTER XII
COUNTRY DOCTORS AND CECILTON DRUG STORE

When I was a small boy sixty plus years ago, the first local Sassafras Neck country doctor that I can remember was Doctor Crawford, who lived just west of Cecilton, on or along the Cecilton/Earleville road. Dr. Crawford owned his farm where he lived, another farm across the road, and another a little east of Cecilton on the Cecilton/Warwick road, and practiced his profession in one of his farmhouses. He was a considerable landowner as well as a doctor of medicine.

From what my elders have said, he stuck to medicine and left the farming to his tenant farmers. Dr. Crawford's son is yet living as of this writing and resides on one of the farms east of Cecilton and oversees the tilling of it, and also the one on the opposite side of the road where his father lived. The third farm east of Cecilton has been in other owners' hands for many years.

Long before I was born, two brothers in the town of Cecilton were very medically minded. One owned and operated a drug store in Cecilton and one was a pharmacist, making up many prescriptions for the Sassafras Neck people in his time. He was yet operating his drug store even in my teen years. His name was John Black, but he was better known as Jonnie Black. He and his helpers also served many a milkshake, soda, and ice cream at his soda fountain. The younger people called him Mr. Jonnie. His brother, Dr. R. M. Black, started his medical career as a veterinarian, then later became a medical doctor for humans, taking up extended medical studies to do so. Dr. Black's office was in Cecilton also. He is deceased for many years, but his daughter still resides in the same house where he practiced medicine.

As I recall Dr. Black made many calls away from his office in his Ford Model-T coupe, attending to many ill people in Earleville and all down in the west end necks—Grove, Pond, Pearce, and Veazey's Necks, and up neck east to Warwick. He delivered many babies including this writer, and my brother and sister. He was a well-liked doctor in his day and time. A lady doctor (Dr. Goodson) also practiced in Cecilton for a few years in the 1930s. She also delivered babies and made house calls as long as she was able to do so.

Another well-liked and very good doctor who served much of the Sassafras Neck community in the 1920s and 1930s and did not live in Sassafras Neck, but over the river in his home and office in Kent County in the town of Galena was Dr. George Jones. (The folks in Galena were in all ways good neighbors with the people of Sassafras Neck.) Dr. Jones kept very busy and was in much demand as a doctor. He loved to chew tobacco and always carried a plug of "Days Work" chewing tobacco in his pocket. Many of us down neck folks went to his office in Galena when necessary, and he made house calls in Sassafras Neck when needed. When this writer was a lad, there were no hardtop roads from Cecilton to Earleville and on down in the necks—there were all dirt roads back then.

In the winter during thawing and freezing the roads got very muddy. Many times in severe cases of sickness the doctors would be met at Earleville (if they could get that far), and carried on down the necks by horse and carriage, buggy, and Dearborns, which were horse drawn wagons with a top and side curtains.

Back in those days the nearest dentists were located up in the county seat at Elkton and over the state line in Middletown, Delaware. The nearest hospital was also located in Elkton and was a three story frame building. Up until I was a young man, the only surgeries that were performed were the removal of tonsils and adenoids, amputations of limbs, and quite a number of appendectomies. When I was a small boy, it would cause quite a stir in the community of Earleville when a person was stricken with appendicitis because peritonitis infection was a dreaded killer in those days. People that had been operated on back then were referred to as having been "cut open." However, today Union Hospital in Elkton is a larger modern brick masonry structure, four stories high, with modern conveniences and equipment.

Just a few years before World War II, the town of Cecilton and the whole of Sassafras Neck was very fortunate to have a young doctor named Wallace Obenshain and his wife locate to Cecilton and set up practice. Just as his practice was growing, World War II came along and eventually he found himself in the Army Medical Corps. However, after the war was over this doctor resumed his practice in the town of Cecilton. Over the years he has not only faithfully served Cecilton and Sassafras Neck, but many people from over the State Line in Delaware, and Kent County and Elkton, Maryland. Dr. Obenshain called on many of his patients who were confined in Union Hospital in Elkton. It might be added that he played a big role in planning and helping to get an organization together to start construction of this fine medical hospital.

Dr. Obenshain has been a very dedicated doctor and also found time to teach an adult Sunday School class in Cecilton Methodist Church and at one time, was on the Cecilton town board. The Doctor and his wife have four sons and one daughter. At this writing one of his sons, also a doctor, along with his wife and child were in Africa serving a three-year stint as medical missionaries to the natives in the area in which they were located.

Dr. Obenshain added even more people to his practice in Cecilton from outside the local community, including many out-of-staters who left the metropolitan areas and settled in and around Sassafras Neck. We all hope that Dr. Obenshain can carry on awhile yet despite his heavy workload.

We will wind up this chapter by remembering and recognizing

the medical aspects of the Sassafras Neck country stores. Most all of the country stores sold a few things for home doctoring. The Earleville store sold quinine pills which many country folks took to break up a cold. Some of the old timers would take quinine with some whiskey, go to bed and proceed to sweat out the cold, and many times it worked.

The country stores all sold many medicated sticking plasters to help with aching back muscles or irritated kidneys. Flax seed was sold for inserting into one's eye to remove stubborn foreign particles. Essence of peppermint, niter, oil of cloves, and paregoric were stocked and used for babies with colic, sore gums from teething, and to put into hollow aching teeth. Castor oil and liver pills were on hand for constipation purposes. Cod liver oil could be bought and in the earlier days many a small school kid had to take a pint during the winter to keep their resistance up to keep from catching cold. Most of these home remedies bought in the country stores were quite effective in doctoring the people of Sassafras Neck.

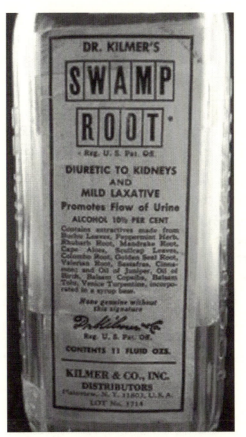

One of the many herbal remedies in the early 1900s

CHAPTER XIII
RELIGION AND JOHNTOWN CHURCH

The history of the churches in Sassafras Neck could be a book in itself. I will henceforth only tell about the locations and the denominations of the Sassafras Neck churches, starting up neck in Warwick, where for many years a Methodist Church stood—a white, wood-frame, country style church that still stands and functions every Sunday and during the week on special occasions such as weddings, funerals, anniversaries, etc. It is kept neat and clean by the members from Warwick and the surrounding area.

About a mile-and-a-half west of the main road between Warwick to Cecilton stands a Catholic Church, St. Francis Xaviour, one of the oldest churches in this country; in its beginning, it was primarily a school for young catholic boys. The church and its accompanying buildings have for some time been restored nicely. The church and buildings are constructed of brick and are now-a-days just used for special occasions. A fairly large cemetery lays on the north side of the church and many old headstone markers date back to the 1700s. Quite often, even today, people get buried there.

In the town of Cecilton stands the Zion Methodist Church, a brick structure with an adjoining building on the west side referred to as the community church house, used for church affairs, Sunday School classes, meetings, church suppers, bazaars, wedding receptions, and the like. Zion is the largest of the Methodist churches in the Sassafras Neck, with a present membership roll of approximately three hundred. A Methodist Church in the black community area of Cecilton joins the property of Zion Church, and it also operates in present times with services every Sunday.

Also, until very recently, an Episcopal Church building stood for many years. It was a small, attractive brick structure with a granite foundation, and in recent years a brick parish building was constructed in back of the church itself, which was demolished in the summer of 1982, thus marking the destruction of another landmark.

About a half mile west of Earleville on Pearce Neck Road stands another very old Episcopal church by the name of St. Stephen's. Much could be written about the history of this church. It is in a beautiful setting. A tree dotted cemetery surrounds the church structure and in recent years was nicely restored. Since the Episcopal Church in Cecilton is now demolished, St. Stephen's holds church services every Sunday. Old and rich in history, St. Stephen's Church goes way back into the very early days of our country.

Another half-mile west on the same road was Johntown St. Paul's Methodist Church, which was among the very first of the Methodist churches to be raised up in this country going back to the day of Charles Wesley and Francis Asbury. The present church building is a neat, country style, white painted clapboard structure built with a bell tower or steeple. This present structure is in a nice shady area and was dedicated in 1893 as a new building. On the west side of the churchyard property is a cemetery with an old church building to one side which is now used as a community building. Everybody fondly calls it the "Old Church," and its cemetery the "Old Cemetery." On the east side of Johntown Church is another cemetery, the present church cemetery. Until more recent years, only four other houses besides the church buildings and property made up Johntown, which has always been surrounded by farmland and still is.

The Methodist Churches of Sassafras Neck are part of the Delmarva Peninsula Methodist Conference. All of my lifetime, both Cecilton Zion Methodist and Johntown St. Paul's Methodist have always been served by the same minister or pastor. The ministers that were appointed by the Peninsula Conference to the various Methodist churches usually stayed for a term of from three to five years, or less if they were not liked by the congregation. The minister's residence for the Johntown church was located on the church property in Cecilton.

When I was a boy, preachers always wore black or very dark gray color suits through the week, but on Sundays in the pulpits they would wear a long black split tail coat made especially for preachers. In those days, the preachers were very fundamental and Bible-oriented and once in a while they would deliver a sermon that would border on Hellfire and brimstone.

The preachers, as they were referred to years ago, would go all through the countryside through the week and visit all the people at one time or another—not only their own particular church members but everyone including Catholic and Episcopal people, and the few that held to no church at all. This traveling was done by horse and carriage, and in this writer's day mostly by Model-T Ford.

Preachers sixty odd years ago operated much differently than they do these days. They went out to the people they knew were sick, or suffering from other troubles. Many times, the preachers' wives would be with them and the preacher and his wife would visit at mealtimes, and especially during the suppertime meal, and the people in the country in those days would most always have the makings of a good meal in their meat-houses and pantries to offer them. Many is the time during my boyhood days when the preacher and his wife would come to our house to have supper. Preachers were often invited by many folks to come visit and have a meal. Many christenings, marriages, and ceremonies took place right in the homes years ago.

The preachers of sixty years ago were a much different breed than the preachers, ministers, and pastors of modern days. Back then in the Johntown Methodist Church, very few of the members were highly educated, most being just plain country people as farm folks, villagers, and fishermen. Most of the older preachers never went to high school and many never finished grade school, however most could read and write and do their necessary figuring enough so that they could take care of the church accounts and other business, read their bibles, and teach Sunday School classes. When I was eight years old, my teacher was a farmer, a big burly man who was the father of five sons and three daughters. I remember to this day what a good teacher he was.

In modern times much money is spent by Methodist Churches on high class Sunday School material and some teachers have complained that it is complicated even to the point where it would almost require a college educated person to teach it. A few Sunday Schools have complained that they do not like some of the newer type "of material, so it would seem that governments, politics, and now even religion are too complicated in these days.

Let us now get ready to go to the Johntown Church on a Sunday afternoon, say back about in 1920s. Of course, the day started at home with clean clothes laid out, and in the morning all shoes had to be shined. Then, the noon-day meal was served. Sunday School started at 2:00 p.m., then church service was from 3-4 p.m. So, clean clothes on, hair combed, off we went.

The Earleville kids often walked the three-quarter-mile stretch to Johntown and we were told we had better be there on time or else we would get punished for loitering along the way. We only walked in warmer weather though. Many of the down neck farm folks in my young days came to church in horse and carriage, a few came in Model-T Fords, one family had a Dodge touring car, another had a Hatfield, and still another had a Maxwell. The horses that pulled the carriages would be lined up along a long hitching rail and tied there under the maple trees. The few automobiles would park in the rear of the churchyard.

Most of the people would arrive early.. The women and small children would usually go on into the church, while most of the men would stand outside and talk, smoke, and chew tobacco until the preacher arrived. Very soon the sexton would ring the church bell, pipes would be dumped out, tobacco cuds spit out, and all would go into the church. Some of the men would take out their pen knives and whittle on sticks while waiting for the preacher to arrive.

In wintertime and bad weather, everyone, upon arriving, would go into the church and be concentrated at the rear where a big potbelly stove would be fired up. Quite often, mostly in hot summer weather, some women like the stouter ones would faint, and due to this, many women carried what was called "smelling salts," which would be stuck under the nose of the fainting person to revive her. In those days, many women wore corsets to make them look not so stout, and many times they laced them up very tight, which some thought, hindered the blood circulation which caused the fainting. Some women could be noticed taking out these little dark green bottles and sniffing them to ward off these fainting spells.

Another common thing in those days, was that young women with babies would breast feed them. Instead of pulling out a bottle of milk with rubber nipples out of their handbags, they pulled a breast out of their dress and fed their babies, and no one thought any embarrassing thoughts about it, as it was the natural way for a young baby to be fed.

In the spring of the year, the pound net fisherman used to come up the bay from Tilghman's Island and set nets for the shad fish and herring, bringing some of their wives and crewmen with them. Many of these down bay folks came to Johntown Church. Some of them even sang in the church choir. The Johntown folks looked forward to having the Tilghman's Island fisher folk join in with them every spring. One of our well-liked preachers, Rev. John Thomas Rowlenson, was at one time a native of Tilghman's Island and served the Cecilton Johntown Charge for four years back in the 1920s. He is now deceased and buried in the church cemetery at Tilghman's.

Once the Sunday School classes were over the service began. After a song by the choir and a scripture reading followed by another hymn sung by the choir and the congregation, the sermon started. My mother, Eva Taylor, was the organist at Johntown Church for twenty-five years. The little organ was a reed type one, and was pumped by the feet of the organist.

The preachers, back in the older days, started their sermons off in a rather natural tone of voice, but as they progressed their voices got louder and louder, and at the peak of their sermons they would be very loud, speaking in almost a shout and roar, and sometimes they even hit the lectern with their fists for emphasis. While this was going on many of the men would loudly say amen. The women would rarely say amen. As the preacher approached the end of his sermon his voice would simmer down and sometimes almost sound like a whisper. The sermon ended with an altar call and the final hymn as the collection plates were passed with the benediction.

Everyone would say goodbye and some of the women would kiss each other at this time. The preacher would shake hands as the people filed out of the church. The people would pile into the carriages and cars and head on home as the church service was over until the following Sunday.

In the early part of the summer, the Johntown Church people would start to get ready for Children's Day. This was an annual Methodist Church affair. This service used to always be held on a Sunday evening. About two weeks before this special night, the children (tots and kids up to twelve years of age) would be given their recitations to speak, which they would memorize. Some would sing and some would be in biblical drills. This would take two weeks of intense practicing before the affair came off. Even much sewing would be done in regards to the children's clothing, especially the girls, as their little dresses would have many ribbons attached here and there. They also wore lots of bows and always patent leather slippers.

Children's Day would draw people from all over the west end of Sassafras Neck. The churchyard would be jammed with horses and carriages, Model-T Fords, and other early makes of automobiles. Many people would show up for this special evening (as on Easter Sunday) who weren't members of the church or otherwise ever came to church. The church would be packed to standing.

The program would start with all the participating children marching up the main aisle of the church to their special seats like a parade. When their names were called out to recite or sing, the children would get up and go up onto the platform in back of the altar to perform. Some would speak for about an hour, reciting the drills and singing, then the children's part was over and the preacher, instead of delivering his usual sermon, would praise the children's good work, say a prayer, and then finally give the benediction after which all would file out of the church. Once out of the church, many people gathered and conversed all around the churchyard, and finally all the families and people would get in their carriages and automobiles and go home.

Another annual affair that took place on a Sunday in late October was referred to as Home Coming. This service would begin at the old Methodist Church building nearby with a noon-day meal. Then there was a special afternoon service with a visiting preacher and an evening service with yet another visiting preacher delivering the sermons. Many times these visiting preachers were at one time the former pastors.

The object of Home Coming Sunday was for people to gather with old friends and relatives who had left the neck area and were living elsewhere—some in the cities, or up country, or over in Delaware. For this affair, the church would be trimmed inside with fall or autumn branches with different color leaves and all sorts of fall flowers. For the evening service, the old kerosene lamps in brackets along the walls were lit,, as there was no electricity in Sassafras Neck back then. This was always a good time of friendship and fellowship.

At this stage, I must say a little bit about my relative Uncle Billy. He was a relative on my mother's side—my grandmother's uncle, or my great uncle. Uncle Billy always came to visit my grandmother, mother, and aunt in the fall of the year and stay two weeks or so. He was a farmer at one time in Sassafras Neck, but later went to live in Queen Anne's County. He had been a widower for many years, but in his old days went to live with a daughter in Philadelphia. Back when I was a boy he was in his seventies or eighties, a self-styled Evangelist type of person and very religious.

So when Uncle Billy showed up in late November, everyone knew that it was time to start attending the Johntown Church Revival meeting. Also, he was quite a hunter and woodsman, and an expert at setting snare traps to catch rabbits, and he would go hunting and trapping as well as evangelizing. He was short and stocky with fair skin and blue eyes. His eyes always seemed to be red and irritated though, and when he stayed at home a few days, every morning before breakfast he would pour a solution into a little eye goblet, sit far forward in a chair with his legs spread apart, place the goblet against his eyeball and throw his head back and hold it until the eye had absorbed the solution. He would do this to both eyes and this was watched with wonderment by my brother and I as small boys.

Uncle Billy also believed that the earth was flat and could not be persuaded that it was round. He always ate a bowl of corn flakes for breakfast, and requested pure cream for them instead of plain milk. He had a small goatee of whiskers on his chin which was stained up much of the time with food drippings. He wore black trousers and a sort of a long black coat when he attended the Johntown Church Revival meetings.

The meetings were usually held the month of November before Thanksgiving, and were evening services that ran for two weeks excluding Saturday nights. Uncle Billy would always sit up on one of the benches near the altar rail, so as to be close by when he felt ready to respond to his feelings. The attendance to these meetings was usually only fair as many people were a little shy about attending.

The service would start and the preacher would preach a conscience-pricking sermon ending with pleas for the people to come forward to the altar to be saved. In the meantime, revival type hymns would be sung along with the organ music in order to try and soften the people up some. Members who had already been saved would wander up and down the aisles and plead with their friends and relatives who had not been saved.

At this time, Uncle Billy would get happy and bound up in front of the altar and sing a revival song all of his own, and he knew many by heart. As a few would venture up to the altar, he would get happier and begin shouting and would pull a handkerchief out of his pocket (which was many times dirty) and wildly wave it back and forth over his head. When the people got up from the altar he would hug them and occasionally would grab one and do a little dance.

One night I remember that three local whiskey-drinking rough necks came to a meeting out of curiosity. Uncle Billy knew who they were and when his opportunity came to evangelize, he sang a song of a dozen or more verses about a terrible tragedy, with one verse ending with "Whiskey Did It All." Unfortunately, it had no effect on the three ruffians. After the revival meeting was over, Uncle Billy would be taken to Middletown, Delaware to the Railroad Station to go back to the home of his daughter in Philadelphia.

Everybody loved him and he loved everybody. He, many times, admonished some men for swearing, drinking, and using vulgar language, but even they did not hold any ill will against him and hoped he would be back the next year. Uncle Billy has long been passed away and rests in the Churchill Cemetery in Queen Anne's County.

The Methodist Churches in recent years do not have the Revival Meetings anymore. Many people in modern Methodism respond to a confession of faith. At the old Revival Meetings many converts were won and truly convicted of their sins and saved. Even some "hard nuts" were turned completely around and lead an entirely different life and a better life today. I believe the Methodist Churches are missing out on a very good opportunity to exercise evangelism and to save souls by not having the revival meetings.

Another event was the Johntown Church Supper back in the 1920s and 1930s. These church suppers were an annual affair in the fall of the year just before Thanksgiving and were held to raise money to help pay preachers' salaries and for church upkeep maintenance. Most of the small town and country churches of the Delmarva Peninsula Conference continue to have these church suppers, even in the modern 1980s.

The men helped when they could but the church women were the organizers and the "backbone" of the yesteryear church suppers. The women at Johntown Church would start to plan for the supper early in October. They would select a chairwoman and other women to take charge of contacting the people in the various areas where they lived to donate various kinds of foods for the supper.

A couple of the churchmen would be appointed to go to Tilghman's Island to get twelve to fifteen gallons of the Tilghman's "select" frying oysters a day or so before the supper so they would be nice and fresh. The men would also help clean up the inside of the old church building, set up tables (planks on trestles), and haul in and stack up firewood by the old black iron stove in the kitchen on which the oysters would be cooked in big black iron skillets. The main dishes for the supper were fried oysters, baked chicken, and baked duck with dressing. Suppers would be served on two nights, mostly Thursdays and Fridays.

The cooking and warming, slicing, and dishing up of food was done in the small kitchen by four or five experienced women and a Negro lady named Charity who was much liked by all. Charity always fried the oysters in the big iron skillets on the black iron stove in fresh hog lard. The women in the kitchen would pat out hundreds of oysters in cracker meal for Charity to fry.

The makeshift tables were set using dishes, knives, forks, and spoons loaned by various church women for the supper occasion. As customers flocked in the smell of frying oysters, chicken, and baked duck with celery, onion, and sage flavored dressings whetted appetites. The food was put on the tables in a family style, all-you-can-eat fashion. There were platters piled high with fried oysters, sliced chicken and duck, dishes piled up with stuffing, mashed potatoes, sweet potatoes, coleslaw, cheese and macaroni, beets, lima beans, snap beans, various types of homemade pickles, jams and jellies, hot rolls and Maryland beat biscuits. In the 1920s and 1930s it would only cost seventy-five cents for all one could eat. You could even buy a big oyster stew for thirty cents.

The old Johntown Church kitchen did not have running water, sink, gas, or electric appliances, yet the women of those bygone years could put out a supper second to none. Most Methodist Church kitchens of today have all of the modern conveniences costing hundreds or thousands of dollars, and they do have some good church suppers, but not like those years ago.

The Sunday School picnic was and still is an annual Methodist affair in the summertime. Back then only a few people in the west end of Sassafras Neck owned automobiles and as a result, most picnics were held on farm lawns. Many of the farmhouses and buildings sat well back away from the roads and this caused the necessity of having lanes leading from the public road to the farmhouse and buildings. These lanes, for the most part, would be lined on either side with shade trees or tall pines. Many times these shady lawns would be chosen for the picnic area.

The farm owner would be contacted to get permission and were usually glad to give their consent. These lawn picnics would take up most of the day. Every family would have their own big clean tablecloths to spread on the grass of the lawn on which they would set out their foods such as fried chicken, potato salad, sliced country ham, pickles, and bananas, with cake and lemonade for dessert. The children would play games, the men would pitch horseshoes, and the women folk would sit and talk.

At midday, they would all eat, sitting on the lawn on blankets. Then later more games and horseshoes were played until about four p.m., then everyone would have homemade cake and lemonade for dessert. After dessert all would pack up and clean up the lawn and go home to milk cows, feed poultry and stock, or work in the vegetable garden.

In the early 1920s, a public bathing beach opened up for business at Grove Point and was called Chesapeake Haven, and it's here that Johntown Church used to hold its annual summer picnic. There were picnic tables in the park where all the food could be spread and you could sit and eat. There were several amusement rides for the kids—a roller coaster, whip, a small sort of coaster called the thriller, a Ferris wheel, a little miniature railroad with a real steam locomotive to pull the train, and of course a merry-go-round. Most all of the rides were only ten cents, except the big roller coaster which was fifteen cents.

Young and old alike looked forward to the Johntown Church picnic. On the day of the picnic, a farmer would usually take a load of children in a large farm truck and other families would follow in their cars. Many friends would also go along with them that did not have automobiles. The caravan extending for miles on the way sometimes looked like a funeral procession, and once in a while someone's auto would have a flat tire, but people fixed their flats right along the road, as they always carried their necessary tools and repair kits. So, after a big day everyone went home tired but satisfied. In recent years the Johntown and Cecilton Churches have combined and have their joint annual picnic in Queen Anne's County at the Peninsulas Conference Methodist Camp, Pecometh, which covers a few hundred acres and borders on the Chester River.

Many changes have taken place in Sassafras Neck in the last thirty-five to fifty years. Living styles have changed along with farming, fishing, education and religion. Even people have changed. Many of the older natives have died and the young natives think, do, and live differently than their parents. In addition, the influx of out-of-state people moving in and settling down has had an effect on the old country style Methodist Religion way of life. The personal touch and old-time fellowship is gone.

The old-time preachers did not think of themselves as professionals, but went out and reached the people, sought out those in need of religious advice and ministered to them. In modern times, it seems that younger ministers expect the troubled to come to them, into the confines of their comfortable offices or studies. Church budgets in current times run into large sums of money, almost more than the small congregations of Sassafras Neck can afford. Fortunately, despite all of this, the three Methodist Churches in Sassafras neck continue to survive and are operating every Sunday.

St. Paul's Methodist Church Johntown near Earleville

CHAPTER XIV
RECREATION OF THE SASSAFRAS PEOPLE

People or relatives from the big towns and cities visiting Sassafras Neck would often ask, "What do you people down in the necks do to have fun?" and "Where do you go?" or "Don't you get awfully bored in the winter time?"

The Sassafras Neck people for the most part were far from being bored and each season held its own recreational activities. In April, when the spring commercial fishing season got under way, folks would get together and have a fish fry; white and yellow perch, pan size rock fish, and river catfish were served along with fresh made cornmeal bread. In four or five adjoining farms or villages, relatives would get together for each fish fry. Much fun was had at these family and friend affairs, as well as plenty of good grub.

Once the wild flowers started blooming in May, many of the women folk would be seen with their children or friends walking along the country roads gathering flowers such as violets, periwinkles, snow-drops, and the sweet smelling honeysuckle blossoms that grew abundantly alongside the roads and hedgerows. Sixty years ago there were no paved or hardtop roads west of the town of Cecilton, just plain old dirt roads. Sometimes the women would also gather many baskets of wild greens along with the flowers such as wild mustard, curly dock, Polk, water cress, shepherd sprouts, and lambs quarter. A pot of mixed greens boiled nice and tender with a piece of home-cured side meat or ham-bone was a fine dish and very much enjoyed by Sassafras Necker's.

In the evenings, many of the men would often gather in certain areas and indulge in the sport of horse cart racing. Many people years ago owned a two- wheeled cart called a dog cart, which was a one passenger, lightweight cart drawn by one horse they used to race. This was a great sport back in those days.

Another pastime for some of the village and farm men in the evenings and off days was pitching horseshoes, which went on in spring, summer and late into the fall. Mostly the pegs were driven into the edge of the grade school grounds across the road from the Earleville store or on the John Taylor store property. I remember one Sunday afternoon several men were engaged in this game when someone showed up with some bootleg whiskey and some of the men got drunk and instead of trying to toss the horseshoes to the pegs, wound up throwing them at each other and this, of course, ended the game for that day.

The younger men and teenage boys would always whip up a baseball team and play against other teams from towns and villages of Sassafras Neck such as, Warwick, Cecilton, Fredericktown, and even as far as Kent County. At one time in the 1920s up into the 1930s, the town of Cecilton had a cracker-jack baseball team that had many victories and belonged to an upper Eastern Shore League playing towns such as Galena, Kennedyville, Chestertown and Rock Hall, all Kent County towns, and Churchill in Queen Anne's County.

Sassafras Neck, being river and bay country, sort of made most everyone a fisherman of some kind. As a result, another great pastime was to go fishing or crabbing on off days. People kept busy most of the time, but never too busy to get in a little fishing and crabbing time now and then in the Bohemia and Sassafras Rivers and creeks. Back in those days, only rich people had pleasure boats and there was no such thing as a marina. Many people did have a rowboat and if you didn't have one you could always borrow one.

In June everyone looked forward to school graduations. and there was always a big turnout of people—parents, relatives friends boyfriends and girlfriends of the graduates.

Folks even used to enjoy sitting on their front porches in the evenings, talking with their neighbors after dark, listening to the "tink-tanks" (small frogs "in the ponds and creeks) watching the moon come up or go down and observing the various constellations and occasional shooting stars. People had no radios or television sets to entertain them but were just content with what they had, and I'm convinced that they had more peace of mind than people today.

In summer, other attractions arose. One big one that the young people and some of the older ones welcomed was the summer opening of a bay resort down in Kent County called Betterton. Usually Memorial Day was the official opening and Labor Day the official closing for the summer season. Back then Betterton was mostly a fishing town, plus it had two piers that extended out into the bay where the sailing schooners and steamboats docked in route to and from Baltimore and Philadelphia to load and unload freight. Betterton a fine sandy bathing beach and several large wood-framed hotels (most of which are demolished and/or in dilapidated condition today) which used to room and board many summer vacationers from the cities. They could swim and lay on the beach in the daytime and eat the very best seafood at night.

For the Sassafras Necker's, the best attraction of all was the Saturday night dances held in the old dance hall on the second story of a sprawled out building which housed concession stands, a duckpin bowling alley, shooting gallery, and a restaurant. When I was but a boy, Sassafras Neck folks used to cross over the mouth of the Sassafras River in power boats from a pier at Grove Point into Betterton to attend the Saturday night dances. (My mother and father did so as young people too.) When I was a teenager, groups of us from the Earleville area would go by automobiles. My first auto was a 1929 Chevrolet coupe and it made many trips to Betterton on Saturday nights.

The dance music would usually be a six or seven-piece band playing a mixture of jazz, foxtrots, and waltzes. (Rock and Roll was unheard of back in those days.) As this story is being written the old dance hall and its accompanying amusements have all been demolished. The old boardwalk along the beach has also been torn away and the old Chesapeake Hotel and restaurant has been demolished to give the waterfront area of Betterton a much different look.

We also used to look forward to steamboat excursions which used to run out of Fredericktown, Grove Point, and Cassidy's Wharf, all on the Sassafras Neck side of the Sassafras River. Most of the excursions were an all-day round trip to Tolchester Beach in Kent County, an amusement park about twenty miles further on down the bay from Betterton. Names of the excursion boats included the Kitty-Night, Annapolis, Louise, and the Emma Giles. Many times the neck people would take a day off and the whole family would go on these excursions to Tolchester. This would be a big all day affair. In the late 1920s and 1930s, occasionally there would be an excursion boat trip form Chesapeake City to Riverview Beach and amusement park over in New Jersey. Also, in the earlier times there used to be moonlight excursions on the bay and dancing aboard boat.

Eventually a public bathing beach and picnic ground called Crystal Beach was developed in the end of Pearce Neck located at Reybold's Wharf at the mouth of the Elk River. This offered a lot of entertainment and relaxation to both the Sassafras Neck people and many out of state folks.

A little later on the adjoining property to Crystal Beach (a farm of approximately 250 acres) also became a bathing beach and was called Crystal Beach Manor. In addition to the public beach, building lots for summer cottages were for sale. A few local people bought lots but mostly they were bought up by city folk from upper Delaware, Pennsylvania, and some from New Jersey and New York. This was when the west end of Sassafras Neck started to be "discovered." But for a few years, the west end country people alone enjoyed their hotdog roasts along the beaches, on fires made with drift wood picked up along the shores.

I can also remember when just a small bit of activity would make a happy summer evening for a family. If one had a farm with an icehouse, all at once the idea would come about to make a freezer of homemade ice cream. The milk would be prepared with fresh blackberries, strawberries, or fresh peaches, or just plain vanilla or chocolate. The father and boys would get a hunk of ice from the icehouse, crack it up to put around the freezing can with salt, and before long the ice cream making would be under way. Sometimes the mother and girls would bake a quick sponge cake to go with the ice cream. Then before long, everyone had a big dish of ice cream and a thick slice of fresh warm cake.

Late summer and early fall was a very busy season in Sassafras Neck as it was corn harvest time. Stock ground wheat fields had to be plowed and planted but before this could take place the corn fodder had to be cut and shucked up. Although the bathing beaches and resorts had all closed just after Labor Day, there was the Everett Theater over the state line in Middletown, Delaware to keep us busy.

Many younger folks, especially courting couples, used to frequent the movies at the Everett since it was the place to go on a date. On a frosty fall night at the movies you were met by the smell of hotdogs, hamburgers, fresh onions, mustard, and chili coming from a small establishment adjoining the theater building operated by two Greek brothers. They could make the best hotdogs and hamburgers, and the movie-goers flocked in. The burgers and hotdogs sold for fifteen cents apiece, sodas for ten cents and a cup of coffee for just five cents.

When I was a boy in knee pants, folks would once in a while go to the Philadelphia Zoo by driving to Middletown, DE, taking the train to Wilmington and then going either by train or by the Wilson Line steamboat into Philadelphia. Folks from Earleville or further on down the necks would have to get up at about 4 a.m. and it would be midnight or after by the time they got home, but even though it was a long day, it was a very satisfying trip for both the children and their parents.

Autumn days also turned the thoughts of men and boys to the hunting season, their guns, and their dogs. In late September, the hunting season would be open for squirrels and sixty or more years ago the woods were full of them. Then late in the fall, the clay pigeon, or blue-rock shooting matches would start and continue once a week mostly on Saturday afternoons until about Christmas time. When I was a youngster, I used to load and spring one of the three traps that threw out the clay saucer shape blue-rocks at which the hunters would shoot. Sometimes, the participants would put up a pot of money for the winner of the match, but mostly they would use either hams or turkeys for prizes. These "shoots" were a big time for the men and boys, and sometimes some of the women folk would come out and watch for a while.

During the month of October, or before the weather got too chilly, there were festivals to look forward to, mainly fundraising affairs hosted by the country grade schools and the churches where homemade ice cream, cake, cookies, and candies were donated and enjoyed.. The down neck Sassafras Neck folks liked these festivals because it gave them a chance to go to the gatherings, sit, talk, and compare farming and other notes from one neck to another, since people from down in Grove Neck might not see some of their relatives or friends from Veazey's Neck or Pearce Neck for weeks at a time. So festivals were always looked forward to with much anticipation.

November was open season for rabbit hunting. Even the rabbit dogs seemed to sense the season and get a kick out of going on the hunt. As the weather got cooler late in the fall, folks would start spending the long evenings in the country stores, and goodness knows there was plenty of entertainment, fun, and fellowship there.

Sixty or more years ago, weather trends were much different than they are now. Between Thanksgiving and Christmas considerable amounts of snow fell and the snow season in the late fall and all winter was a time for sleighing and sledding. Many people had horse drawn sleighs. This was a great sport and was a favorite with among young people and courting couples, but some older folks also used to like sleighing. One would have to dress warm, wear mittens, cover up ears, and wrap up in a big heavy robe or blanket to keep knees and legs warm. Sleigh bells could be heard jingling all up and down the west end of Sassafras Neck. Ice skating was also enjoyed by the children and young people. There used to be a big pond in a field on the east edge of Earleville which would be frozen all winter long, and we kids of Earleville played on it often in the evenings.

Another spot was the old mill pond down along Sandy Bottom Road. It was much larger than the Earleville pond and was very good for skating due to its size. Youngsters and grown-ups from Earleville, Fredericktown, and Cecilton used to congregate at this mill pond to skate. Many years ago, it was bought by an out-of-state man for the purpose of fish farming to grow fish to stock others ponds and that ended the skating parties down on the mill pond. But while they lasted, the winter sports of skating, sledding, and sleighing afforded much fun and entertainment in the winter time.

After the Christmas and New Year's holidays were over, there would be old time square dances in many of the big old farmhouses. Jim the fiddler and Charley the banjo player would be engaged to play the music and many couples would attend, young and old. Back in those days, a little "bootleg" whiskey would get mixed up with the dancing, and sometimes tempers would flare up over girlfriends and fist-fights would break out, but regardless of a fight now and then, it was a good pastime on winter nights.

Then, occurring quite often in all seasons of the year were parties for young newlyweds called "showers," where you went and took a gift that would help the young couple to get started with housekeeping. Gifts would consist of pots, pans, dishes, towels, rugs, and other things necessary for the house. After the opening of gifts, there would be cake, lemonade, and coffee for refreshments. There were also many birthday parties.

The people of the west end of Sassafras Neck had and did many things that would keep them entertained and free from boredom all year long. Indeed, even their work, with the spirit of helping one another, had some pleasure in it. Back then people in the necks or just country people in general seemed to be more content and live much happier and satisfied lives than people of today.

Now-a-days, people have so much to entertain them—luxury cars, TV's, radios, electrical appliances, stereo music, and just about every gadget that can be thought of, but the more they have, the more they want.

Back years ago, there was a little "boot-leg" whiskey, a fist-fight now and then, and some minor thieving, but very little crime as compared to what goes on in present times with all the liquor stores, booze joints, and dope-rings causing trouble, not only with young people but also with many older people who should know better than to do some of the crazy things they do.

I hope in this chapter one can get some idea of how the country people of Sassafras Neck entertained themselves and, for most, lived contented, satisfied, and unselfish lives. They worked hard and had trials and tribulations of all kinds, but learned and knew how to "roll with the punches."

The Boardwalk at White Crystal Beach in Earleville

Tolchester excursion steamer "Louise" ticket

CHAPTER XV
THE ECONOMIC DEPRESSION

In the month of October, 1929, Wall Street and the stock market took a bad tumble, and shortly thereafter the whole nation was beginning to feel the effects of a terrible economic depression that did not let up or start to improve much until the late 1930s. Much could be written about this terrible depression and indeed there has been, so we will not, in this writing, dwell on the whys and wherefores of it. However, the depression did very greatly affect the Sassafras Neck people—every man, woman, child, farmer, tradesman, waterman and business owner.

The people in Sassafras Neck who had been able to save some money and put it in the hands of the local banks lost a lot of money. Most of the neck banking was done at the Cecilton Bank, which was a branch bank of the Elkton Bank and Trust Co. The savings mostly went into bank selected investments and when the Elkton Bank and

Trust Co. went under, as many banks across the nation did, many people lost their savings. Most hard hit, financially speaking, were the prosperous farmers and the business establishments. Many retired farmers lost practically all their savings.

    This sad event shortened the lives of some of the old folks. It also complicated things for the young farmers, and some of the less fortunate had to give up and quit farming, as they were unable to meet the demands of fertilizer, seed company, farm machinery and equipment repair bills, and were also unable to meet the demands of the Health Department in regard to the dairy part of farming. The wheat crop of 1930 brought less than a dollar a bushel, and at that price, the farmers did not break even when they deducted for the price of fertilizer, their labor, and wear and tear on their farm equipment.

When farming went down in Sassafras Neck everything else suffered because farming was the backbone of the Sassafras Neck economy. So by the middle of 1930, everyone was beginning to run out of money and by the end of 1930 everyone was complete out of cash money. Most of the farmers could not afford to keep hired help because they had no money to pay the wages. Just about all of the tradesmen were out of work, as no one could afford to have any kind of repair work done. The small country business establishments such as shops, stores, and gas and repair stations were hard hit and many of them folded up. Many people were given credit by these businesses, all hoping that recovery would be occur soon; however it didn't, and some of the small businesses went broke due to the over-extension of credit.

    My own grandfather was a typical example of a victim of the mishandling of older people's money and savings. He was a retired farmer and owned a moderate size farm near Earleville free and clear. He was a fairly prosperous farmer and had worked hard all his life. Much of his savings was in the hands of the Elkton Bank and Trust Co. The bank, of course, invested money and much was invested in a twenty-year maturity type of bond. He also had approximately three-thousand dollars in a savings account in the Cecilton branch bank, which he himself never saw again. The bonds never paid off to any extent.

    I can remember one evening he received a letter from out in the

Midwest from some firm's attorney. In the letter was a check for one-hundred and two dollars, as the company involved in the bond had gone bankrupt, so that was what he received for one-thousand dollars invested for twenty years. When I read the letter to him, he never blinked an eye, changed his expression, or made any outrageous statement, but the old man was hurt. His salvation was that he had a savings of about four thousand dollars in a bank in Middletown, DE that did not go broke. He still owned his farm, his home in Earleville, and in his later years worked for the State Road Commission of Maryland. He lived to be pretty old (eighty-five years). A couple of years before he died he sold his farm for three-thousand, three hundred dollars. Today, in the 1980s, the same farm would bring a hundred-thousand dollars or more.

My old grandmother lived on for several years, with her daughter, to age 98. By that time, the money from the sale of the farm and the money in the sound bank in Middletown was used up. About the only thing left was her home in Earleville, which my aunt inherited at my grandmother's death.

The Sassafras Neck people, of course, managed to endure and survive the depression. Since there was no money to speak of, people began thinking, regardless of the lack of money, we still have to eat. The farm folks, of course, had wheat and corn that was worth nothing on the market but they could have it ground up into flour and cornmeal. They had cows for milk, hogs for meat, potatoes from the truck patch, plus other vegetables which the womenfolk canned for winter use.

But the money they received from the sale of grain and milk was not enough to pay the expenses of raising the crops or for cow feed. So farmers had to go further in debt every year of the depression and many quit and had to declare bankruptcy. The townspeople of Earleville were hit especially hard. Most all of the Earleville families had gardens for vegetables, a pen in which they could raise a couple of hogs for meat, and most had a small poultry house for chickens and ducks, so at least the townspeople had something to eat, but very little, if any, money for groceries such as bread, sugar, tea, and coffee. There were times when the farmers just had to have help, like during the wheat and corn harvests, so many of the town and village people would work for the farmers at these times, and what little money they received would at least buy some coffee, tea, sugar, cornmeal and a pair of shoes now and then.

A typical wage for wheat harvesting in the early 1930s was just three dollars a day and those work days were ten and twelve hours long. For cutting corn fodder, the wage was ten to twelve cents a shock, and for husking out the ears of corn, forty cents a barrel.

I was lucky enough to get a job driving a milk truck. I used to start on the job at 6 a.m. and start picking up milk from various Sassafras Neck farmers. A usual load consisted of about 150 steel cans that held eighty-five pounds of milk each, which I hauled to a Mount Pleasant, DE creamery. After unloading the cans, they were emptied and steamed inside, then hauled back to the farmers for the next day's milking. My milk route run would usually be finished at noon. It was a seven-day-a-week job and my wages were one dollar a day. The rest of the day for quite a while (my young wife Susie, the baby and myself were living with my wife's aunt and uncle on a farm in Grove Neck) I worked on the farm in exchange for a place to stay and food for myself, my wife, and our baby.

Many people traded work for wood to burn in their heaters. The people of Sassafras Neck more or less helped each other by trading about for wood, corn or wheat, and sometimes hog meat. In the depression days, not too many women smoked, but for the men who smoked cigarettes, a 15-cent package of cigarettes was too much money, so many bought a five cent bag of Dukes Mixture of Bull Durham with the cigarette papers attached and rolled their own. Many bought corn-cob pipes and ten cent cans of pipe tobacco. Finally, a depression cigarette hit the market for ten cents for a pack of twenty and many reverted back to the tailor mades.

For the men who liked a drink of whiskey now and then, there were a few whiskey stills down in the west end necks, and some bootleg whiskey could be had at a moderate price. It used to be called "white-mule" whisky, as most of it had not aged long enough to attain the proper amber color. Many of the upper county people used to frequent the whiskey still sites. During the depression the bootleggers had more money than anyone else in Sassafras Neck, and they were the few people who could afford a new car. The bootleggers always bought the bigger, faster cars so they could out-run the sheriffs and motorcycle mounted state-troopers. A few times, the County Sheriff at Elkton and his deputies, along with federal agents, would get a lead on the location of a still in Sassafras Neck, make a raid and blow up the still, and mash barrels and other equipment. This would make for a lot of excitement around the countryside and much discussion at night in the Earleville country store. Later on in the 1930s, the prohibition of alcohol ended and legal beer, wine, and whiskey establishments began to open here and there, and the bootleggers slowly went out of business.

During the depression, a few fellows who were good at fixing automobiles (auto mechanics) did really well financially speaking. People who had automobiles (with the exception of the few people fairly well fixed financially) did not have the money to buy new cars. Indeed, many hardly had the money to get repair work done. As a result, everyone tried to keep his old auto running so these few mechanics did much work on the repair of these autos to keep them going, and made fair wages for doing this. People many times did not have the money to buy new tires, and kept using their old tires until they were threadbare by using various types of blowout patches. There were no tubeless tires in those days, so everyone carried the tube patching kits and blowout patches.

Gasoline, many times, could be bought at six gallons for a dollar. Cheap grades of cylinder oil were fifteen cents a quart, higher grades were twenty cents a quart. Oil that was drained out of crank cases was saved and recycled. This was done by straining dirty oil that was drained out of crank cases through about four different pieces of burlap bag material; this really did clean up the dirty oil to a good extent, as it took out the dirt and sludge from the old drained oil.

In the late 1930s, things in general began to look up and the economy started to pick up a bit. Farmers had begun to get better prices for milk and grain. People were slowly beginning the climb out of debt. In 1938 and 1939, the second World War was getting underway in Europe, and this was starting to help many factories in the nearby cities and larger towns such as Wilmington, DE, Chester, PA and Elkton and Chestertown, MD.

Then on December 7, 1941 the Japanese attacked Pearl Harbor and the US declared war on Japan. When this happened, the factory wheels across the nation began to turn faster. Old established shipyards began to work full blast and yacht yards soon turned into sizeable shipyards building all kinds of marine craft for the Army and

Navy. Airplane factories were enlarging and expanding to build planes for the US Air Force, the Army, Navy, and Coast Guard. Munitions factories were blooming here and there. The Roosevelt administration was calling for action and cooperation between industry and labor and they really got it.

Most everyone in the Sassafras Neck area (as in other areas of the nation) began to put the great economic depression behind them. Most everyone had a job in a factory or a nearby shipyard and this was what sent many of the Sassafras Neck women to work. Just about everyone was in the war effort in some way. The farmers were also doing better, as crop and milk prices increased. As the old saying goes, "wars are and have always been good for economies." Sad but true. The war and war efforts did end the depression for the most part, however it also was the beginning of many radical shifts that changed the lifestyle of the people of Sassafras Neck.

As this is being written, people of today who are forty-years-old or less do not know about or realize the effects of the great depression. Many of the higher educated ones have, of course, studied about it. When some of us older people who went through the depression tell our children or other younger people about it and our experiences, they find it hard to believe, as they have grown up in fairly prosperous times. Even many young teenagers of today go to high school in their automobiles and motor bikes. They attend many functions which did not exist in older days. There are larger (and I hope, but sometimes doubt) better schools being built everywhere. There seems to be much more emphasis on education.

The Great Depression of late 1920s and early 1930s did cause many hardships, but the people of Sassafras Neck did learn how to do without many things and how to make do with what little they had.

Necessary rest facilities at Johntown St. Paul's Church before indoor plumbing

CHAPTER XVI
WAR EFFORTS IN WORLD WARS I AND II

This writing would not be complete without more mention of World Wars I and II. I was a small boy in the days of the U.S. involvement in World War I, but there are a few things that I can remember about it. According to history, on April 2, 1917, the President of the United States, Woodrow Wilson, asked Congress to vote on a declaration of war against Germany as their submarines were wreaking havoc on U.S. shipping all over the Atlantic, causing great losses of men, ships, and goods. Congress voted for a declaration of war against Germany by an overwhelming majority and the President signed the declaration on April 6, 1917.

As a result, men across the nation were required to register, and three to four million men were soon drafted and many willingly enlisted. Quite a few men from the west end of Sassafras Neck were drafted. Up until the time of this war business, things had been going along in the neck in a fairly prosperous and normal sort of way. However, I can remember even before the U.S. involvement that people were reading in the newspapers about the German warfare against US shipping.

So the war was just about the biggest topic of discussion most anywhere in Sassafras Neck. I can remember on one occasion my father had to go to Wilmington, DE to get certain supplies for the blacksmith and wheelwright businesses that he and his brother operated. On this trip he took Mom, my brother, and me with him. While in the city he took us to a movie theatre (which was my first time in a movie theatre). During the show, at one time, they showed some pictures of a submarine, explosions and the sinking of a U.S. ship. This frightened my brother and me and we had to leave the theatre.

Also, somewhat before and during the U.S. involvement, there was much discussion of and about German spies. The grownups, young people and children all seemed to dread the possibilities of running up against these types of people. Before any of the actual war activity, anyone that drifted into the neck whom the local people did not know were referred to as strangers, but during the war they were referred to as spies and the neck people would be very reluctant to have anything to do with them. Many of the neck people were more shy of these so called spies than they were of occasional bands of gypsies that used to occasionally visit the necks.

Once in a while, a large Army balloon would get loose from the Army Proving Grounds in Aberdeen, MD across the bay and drift over the bay to the west end of Sassafras Neck and get hung up in a woods among the trees, and this caused great excitement up and down the countryside, as some folks thought that maybe a spy had been in it and maybe was on the loose somewhere in the necks.

U.S. Army planes were just beginning to get advanced enough so that they could be used against German planes in Europe. Once in a while, one of these planes would fly across the bay over to the Sassafras Neck area, fairly low, and that would stir up the people, as their minds at that time of the war were very German and spy conscious.

Most of the men of the Sassafras Neck area who were drafted and called to fight in the war were very patriotic and did want to fight for their country. However, a very few did not see it that way. A few times someone would try to dodge the draft by hiding in the woods or in a barn or stable when he thought some Army official was due to come after him. Another way to dodge the draft was to turn to farming, as there were many exemptions pertaining to farmers. By and large, the draft dodger type of men were in a very small minority in the necks. Sassafras Neck was very well represented by their soldiers in World War I, for the size of the area and the population at that time.

No sooner had war been declared then music and songs were coming out, patriotic and attuned to the war and our fighting men who were arriving in Europe. Such songs included "Keep the Home Fires Burning," "Parlez-vous," and "When the War is Over, Over There," and others.

During the U.S. involvement, homes and schools were urged to knit wool squares (about a square foot) with olive drab army color wool. Mothers and children were busy knitting in the evenings at home, as many sons, brothers, and other relatives were fighting in the war. The Earleville grade school teacher even had a knitting period in school for the pupils who knew how to knit. Also, the school children were asked to save all the hulls from nuts and bring them into school to be collected by Army officials, as they would be made into fiber that was necessary for the making of gas masks to withstand the mustard gas attacks on our soldiers in Europe. The woolen knit squares would be made into blankets to keep our soldiers warm in the battle camps. Also, tinsel-paper, like the kind used to wrap chocolate bars, was another item to be collected. When a family got enough together to roll up into a ball the size of a tennis ball, that too was taken to the collection center to be picked up by the officials.

The big shipyards were building ships to replace those that had been sunk by German subs and to carry grains and food-stuffs to war torn Europe. General John J. Pershing and his valiant men did some hard, tough fighting in Europe and in the war against Germany and finally, the "Kaiser" had been won, the Armistice was signed, and the U.S. soldiers were getting ready to come back home.

During the war, wages for workers went up. Farmers got more for their grain, as it was much in demand in Europe to feed people in the war torn areas. During the winter of 1918, most of the men who fought overseas in Europe arrived home. The soldiers from the west end of Sassafras Neck all got back safe, however two of my father's men did have some trouble. One lost his right arm up to the shoulder, and the other got a nasty dose of German mustard gas.

Another of my father's men came to our house at the farm to visit us soon after he got home. He thought it would be fun to appear with his gas make on. (The gas masks of World War I, when in place on the person's face, looked almost exactly like an elephant's snout or trunk.) As my brother and I were yet small boys, this gas mask attire startled us very much until we found out it was dad's friend. Dad's friend who was seriously affected with mustard gas is still living as the story is being written (1980s) and is in his eighty-sixth year. Also, the only other living WWI veteran from the west end of the neck is a black man, Clarence Price (nicknamed "Rabbit") who is close to 90 years of age and still does some light work cutting grass with his power riding mower, cleaning up leaves and gardening for many folks in the Cecilton area, both black and white.

At this point, a little should be written about the period of time between WWI and October 1929. Economically speaking, this was a good and fairly prosperous time in Sassafras Neck. Farming was the basic economy of Sassafras Neck and the farmers, during most of the time from 1918 to 1928 and 1929, were still getting good prices for their grain, milk, and other farm products as much of it was in demand for the recovery of war ravished Europe.

As the farmers were doing well, so were all other businesses, as they mostly served the farmers. People in general were in good spirits over the war victory and most were happy about the League of Nations organization, as they thought this would outlaw all wars and thus provide lasting peace and they would hear no more of fathers, brothers, relatives, and friends having to go to war.

The farms still retained their herds of horses, but many could afford and did buy tractors to pull plows and other farm equipment, which did lighten their work. Most families had an automobile of some sort. In the ten or so years of 1918 to 1929, there was a general air of good feeling and fairly good, prosperous times, which suddenly came to an end when the Depression struck in October 1929.

Let's skip now to the year 1939 when Nazi Germany started their great and terrible army, going into adjoining countries and taking over—their governments. their people, their business, and everything else—and subjecting the people of these smaller countries to their murderous iron-fisted rule, thus starting World War II against France, Poland, Denmark, the Netherlands, and eventually England.

On December 7, 1941, the Japanese attacked the Pearl Harbor US military base, causing great loss of U.S. Navy war battleships and many lives (approximately 2,300 Navy personnel, other military personnel, and civilians). President Franklin D. Roosevelt, with Congress, immediately declared war on the nation of Japan. This aligned the United States with Great Britain, France, Russia, and other European allies. Germany was already aligned with Japan and Italy, and this set the stage for an around the world war known as World War II.

Again, U.S. men were required to register and soon many men were being drafted for military duties. President Roosevelt called on the nation to cooperate as fully as possible to put forth a great war effort. Now that the United States had declared war on Japan, a much greater effort was needed. Many training camps and schools were needed here and there across the nation to train men for duty in the Army, Navy, Air Force, and Coast Guard. Many men who were too old to be drafted worked in shipyards which were all operating full blast to build warships, merchant ships, and many types of smaller crafts to be used in amphibious landings against the enemy. Many carpenters, tradesmen, and laborers, worked on the construction of Army and Navy training camps night and day to complete them as soon as possible.

One such place was the Bainbridge Naval Training Station just inside the mouth of the Susquehanna River nearby the town of Port Deposit, MD. When completed, this training base could house, feed, and train approximately 30,000 men, plus many women WAVES, in many types of duties as sailors. This writer took boot camp training at Bainbridge and then spent sixteen weeks in the navy Quartermaster school also at Bainbridge, which basically taught piloting, seamanship, and navigation. It was amazing how much had been accomplished for the war effort, even by the end of 1942.

Similar activities were going on all over the nation. During the war, a small fire cracker plant in Elkton, MD soon expanded and developed into a large munitions plant. This plant manufactured bullets, and 20 and 40 mm anti-aircraft shells for the Navy. Many women and men of the Sassafras Neck area worked in this plant during WWII—mothers, daughters, and wives of the men who were in the war in Europe and in the Pacific areas, including my wife Susie—and they felt duty bound to help their sons and husbands win the war. Older men, and men not physically fit for drafting also worked in plants to help the war effort. Many men from Sassafras Neck fought in WWII, in all branches of the service and all around the world.

Not too long after the United States entered the war, it became necessary for the Federal Government to put certain foods and gasoline on a ration system. In July 1942, gasoline ration stamps/coupons were issued in a small booklet form in which so many stamps were enclosed. They lasted for a certain period of time and when the time period ran out, another book would be issued and so on.

Many people thought that through favoritism, crooked dealing, and bribing, many other people managed to get more than their lawful share of ration stamps. During this period of rationing many automobile gasoline tanks were drained at night by thieves and of course, this was going on all over the country. Sugar and coffee was on rations, but black market operators always managed to have some at extra high prices; this always happens in war times. Most people are patriotic, in the military service, or join the effort on the home front, but there are always a few low-down curs that think only of themselves and the fast easy money they can make.

After the Normandy Beach landings and other subsequent victories in Europe, Germany signed an unconditional surrender to the allied nations on May 6, 1945. At about this time, Japan was going downhill fast, and on August 6, 1945, the first atomic bomb ever to be used was dropped on the Japanese city of Hiroshima, destroying much of the city and killing approximately 80,000 people outright, injuring thousands more. On August 9, three days later, the second atomic bomb was dropped on the city of Nagasaki, with much destruction and loss of life. This was the end of the war with Japan, and on September 2, 1945, General MacArthur and Admiral Nimitz received Japan's surrender onboard the battleship Missouri in Tokyo Bay, thus ending World War II.

Again, as in WWI, the fighting men were coming home and in a few months most had returned, but this time a few of the Sassafras Neck men didn't make it. Some lost their lives in Europe action, others in the Japanese Pacific action. Our World War II President F.

D. Roosevelt died suddenly on April 12, 1945, and this shocked the nation. Vice-President Harry Truman stepped up and he inherited the war to finish and made the hard decision to drop the atomic bombs on Japan. In addition to this, President Truman had to contend with the Korean War. We will end this chapter at this point and go to the post World War II days in the following chapters.

World War II soldiers from 29th Infantry Division leave Elkton Armory for deployment

CHAPTER XVII
THE ENDING OF OLD TIME FARMING AND LIFESTYLE

In the neck, farming of the land was the main part of the economy and a year-round activity, and as such it had the most influence of anything on the kind of country living that the neck people used to enjoy.

Of course, there were other types of employment and work in the neck, such as fishing, carpentry, saw mills, grocery stores, hardware stores, and in later years, filling stations and garages, but even then, most of these non-farming jobs were related to the backbone business of farming. By and large, the neck people were all inter-related job wise and occupation wise, and most all were satisfied with their lot, as life in Sassafras Neck and especially the west end area was unhurried; people were more or less independent, everybody knew everyone else, and people were friendly to one another.

As always, and as everywhere else, there were, of course, a few disgruntled folks here and there. After the terrible economic depression of 1929 and into the 1930s, things began to happen to start changing the way of the necks in regard to the agricultural farming business, which greatly affected the lifestyle of the Sassafras Neck people and is still affecting it even as this is being written.

As mentioned in a previous chapter, the method of farming was the five-field rotation tillage method for farming corn, wheat, and other grains and crops and dairy farming. Most every farmer depended on his dairy cattle and milk production for a monthly cash income, which supplemented income in between the annual moneys derived from the grain crops. However, and for some time, medical people were blaming a lot of the cases of tuberculosis (TB) on the milk coming from the small dairymen, so a war was waged, so to speak, on the small dairymen. Milk cow herds, by law, had to be TB tested.

As a result, many of the less able farmers lost most of their cows, as they failed the test, and cows were also lost by the more able farmers. Some of the smaller farmers almost immediately went out of business, as they could not recover financially from the loss. In the late 1920s and on into the 1930s, some sold out, quit farming, and moved off and away. The larger and better off financially farmers continued to hang on, but were continually being told by health officials to build milk houses with coolers installed, remodel cow sheds and milking stables, and many more minor things until it got to the point that ultimately one had to change his farming style and only concentrate on dairy farming.

So, little by little, the combination method of crop and dairy farming was being squeezed out by the requirements of the Board of Health, which was in turn being pressured by the big dairymen in other states. It certainly did put a big crimp in the Sassafras Neck type of farming. No doubt, tubercular cattle and unsanitary conditions did contribute to the tuberculosis disease, but it was sad to see so many farmers give up and quit. Some, or at least a few of the smaller farms actually did start to grow into scrub brush, as they were vacant for long spells of time.

As of today, and in all of Sassafras Neck, there is not one farmer or farm that is being tilled or crop farmed as in the former days of yesteryear. Only a few of the original type of Sassafras Neck farmers are in existence today (the 1980s) on farmland. They are either strictly dairy farmers or have gone into beef cattle.

While a lot of these changes and farming difficulties were taking place, Sassafras Neck was also being "discovered," so to speak, by out of state people—who were discovering not only the neck, but the entire Eastern Shore of Maryland. As a result, one could see realty signs going up in every town more and more as time went on. In order to try to keep on farming, some local farmers tried (and some are still trying) to till more acreage and plant more land in grain, such as corn, wheat and soybeans, trying to hang in by increasing the volumes. Some farmers today are tilling hundreds of acres of farmland, and a few are farming a few thousand acres. Many are leasing or renting ground to till.

But many of the local farmers who gave up a few years back put their farmland up for sale and sold-out to mostly out of state land speculators, who moved in for the "kill," buying up all the Sassafras Neck land they could get their hands on, working, of course, very closely with the dozens of realtors located in the upper bay country, who all sit around waiting for local farmers or landowners to give up and quit farming or die of old age so that their farmland can be put up for sale and sold.

Many times, the farm owner's heirs would rather turn the land over to a realtor to sell in a booming land market for a big profit rather than continue to till the land themselves. The two hundred to four hundred acre family farms in Sassafras Neck, for the most part, have just about passed away—a fallen victim to big business farming. This sort of thing has happened to many farming communities, especially in the Middle Atlantic area of the East Coast. Much US farmland in the later 1970s and early 1980s was sold to foreign interests.

It is sad and wrong for any kind of business in this nation to fall prey to big business and/or big operators. Will Rogers once said, "When you see a bunch of outsiders beginning to come and go in and out of a community or county, right then you all better get ready to sign some deeds. The outsiders don't come in for nothing—none of them. Investment is two jumps away from control by strangers in a community. They next move is more or less permanent and before you know it, they have everything under their control and you, the original owners, have nothing to say about anything."

This is what is happening in Sassafras Neck at the present time.

Many of the land speculator types who purchase land will either till or rent the ground out to local farmers to till, to pay the county taxes on their newly acquired land. Many times, the original barns, sheds, stables, and even farmhouses will be demolished or burned to keep away from upkeep and to cut down on the county tax assessment. Valuable hedgerows get torn out to gain a few extra bushels of grain or soybeans.

Farmland stands of woods have also been ravished by loggers. Enough wood has been wasted by loggers to keep a small town in heating fuel for years. After cutting out the trunk sections of a tree, the tree tops with all the smaller limbs just lay around all over the woods and rot. Logging operations with their large heavy equipment, make deep ruts all over the woodland areas. These ruts fill up with rainwater, which in summertime gets stagnant and breeds mosquitoes. So, from the foregoing, one can see how the once good family type farms are falling prey to greedy speculators and realtors to be ripped and ravished by loggers, big operator types of land tilling equipment, and various developers.

Gone is the day of the individual and family type farms of Sassafras Neck, with their mixed breed type of dairy herds pasturing in the fields. No more are the shocks of corn fodder in rows across the fields with the green blanket of winter wheat coming up through the freshly tilled earth. As before stated, much of the farmland of Sassafras Neck has been sold to the outlander speculators. Some have bought up as many as one or two farms, some as many as six or seven adjoining farms. Big business and big operators have just about consumed the family type farms in the neck. The land is plowed up and saturated with chemical type fertilizers. Some scientists seem to think that eventually the chemicals will kill the ground topsoil, as all of nature's underground workings of worms and various types of beetles and insects (which keep the ground somewhat opened and aired) will be killed off by the harmful chemicals.

The modern type of farmer seems to care little for what might be happening to the land. Their greed for more and more bushels of this or that comes first. It is very sad to see how the once beautiful Sassafras Neck farms, woods, and streams have been mangled up by big operators.

There are a few reasons to explain the plight of Sassafras Neck farmland. As already mentioned, the type and style of farming has radically changed. Of course, much more grain per acre has been yielded. Much of the larger yields came about because of the demand for grain, beans, and other farm products in foreign countries who were willing to pay top prices for these farm products, which in turn has driven the prices for food sky high for the American people. Another reason for the demise of the local farmer and his farmland property, is the fact that the younger generations of the local farmer's children are more highly educated than their parents and grandparents and will not lend themselves to farm work and the responsibilities that go with it. It was a good life for their elders, but many of the younger ones don't see it that way.

Yet another reason is that even though a few of the younger people would like to farm, the farming business has now become a big operators game and is too costly an industry to get into, with farm machinery currently costing (early 1980s) as much as fifty thousand dollars or more for big equipment such as diesel tractors, combines for the harvesting of grain, and large trucks to haul the grain to the storage areas.

Still, another reason for the fading of Sassafras Neck farming is the fact that the currently high and ever-increasing prices for land tempt some of the younger heirs of farmland to sell out and get (to use an old expression) "filthy rich overnight." Sadly, as has often been the case, the parents worked a lifetime to pay for and own their farm, and did without many things to do so in order to have something to leave for their children—only to have it sold for big money soon after they are gone. The heirs could care less how hard their parents have strived, wanting only to live it up on the proceeds of big money land sales.

However, there are a few of the younger farmers in the Sassafras Neck area who have managed to "hang-in" and are making out very well by their own wisdom and good management. A few have turned strictly to the raising of beef cattle such as Black Angus and the Hereford mostly. The grain these fellows raise mostly goes back into the feeding of the cattle. Others have gone in to raising dairy cattle herds (thoroughbreds) for dairy farming and milk. Still, others raise dairy herds to sell to cattle dealers. Some of the local farmers who own their farms continue to grow grain and soybeans and, in addition, will rent ground to grow corn and other grain which increases their volumes, and in that way will be able to make it farming.

And so it is now with farming in Sassafras Neck, that for the most part, people either get big or else get out, because agricultural and farming is getting to be such a big business. Many would not like to have to go into big operations but are forced to if they want to continue farming, and this is sad because pure greed is the father of big business.

Modern harvesting equipment

CHAPTER XVIII
REALTORS, DEVELOPERS, AND RADICAL CHANGE

Before World War II, there were no real estate offices in the towns of Cecilton, Warwick, Earleville, and Fredericktown, or indeed anywhere in the confines of Sassafras Neck. The sale of the land, farms, or residential properties were handled by the owners themselves, who sold directly to the individual or individuals themselves, who were in most cases friends. Sometimes, in later years, an owner would place his property into the hands of a real estate agent. Thirty or more years ago, in the larger outlying towns out of the limits of Sassafras Neck such as Elkton, Chestertown, or Middletown, and even in the larger cities and towns at that time, realtors still weren't too numerous.

Then, after World War II when things had gotten somewhat settled down from all the war action, a great cry arose across the nation proclaiming a great housing shortage. This started up a great effort by many developers to buy up land all over whenever and wherever they could so they could build houses; these tracts of land were, of course, referred to as housing developments. In turn, real estate agent offices started springing up. A big "band-wagon" so to speak had started moving, and the realtors jumped on it.

At the present time there are four real estate offices operating in the town of Cecilton alone. To give the reader an idea of the extent of the realtor boom, we must go a few miles beyond the extent of Sassafras Neck. At the present time (1980s) the Kent County News weekly paper is showing listings of twenty or so realtor agencies, of which five or so are located just over the river in the town of Galena. There are a half-dozen just over the state line in the town of Middletown, DE, ten miles east of Cecilton. There are three or four in Chesapeake City, eleven miles north of Cecilton. In the Cecil Whig weekly paper, there are listings of thirty or more realtors located in and around Elkton. So, this gives you an idea of how the Sassafras Neck area and the surrounding communities are saturated with realtors who have succeeded in convincing most people into believing that they are an absolute necessity concerning the buying or selling of property.

So now realtors are making money buying and selling properties which used to be handled by the buyer and seller themselves making their own private transaction with no fees involved. In the Cecilton, Sassafras Neck area, the four agents who have had a Realtor office here for twenty years originally came from another state. Still, another from out of state has been operating here for four years. Many of the realtors who operate in Cecil County, upper Kent County, and in the head of the bay area in general, are from out of the state. Many of these operators manage to get a hold of local properties and come bargaining in, uninvited, and set up shop which, of course, there is no law against. This is not very good for the local people who are in the real estate business. This big real estate business, mostly, has taken place in the last quarter century, especially in the last twelve or fifteen years. The real estate boom certainly is not confined to the Sassafras Neck area, but is now nationwide in choice areas across the country.

The largest town in Sassafras Neck is Cecilton, followed in size by Warwick, Hacks Point, Fredericktown, and Earleville. These small towns were originally defined by two or three houses and a store or a sort of a hotel in colonial times, more or less, with the exception of Hacks Point which, sixty years ago, was nothing more than a big briar patch between the Bohemia River and Scotsmen's Creek; although it started out with a few people buying lots and building summer cottages, it slowly developed into a year-round residential area that even has its own fire company. The other above-mentioned towns have developed slowly and normally and are not at this time overdeveloped, and they are occupied mostly by the local people and their dependents or relatives.

There are a few developments in the neck that have really grown since World War II. West View Shores was once a prosperous farm, lying between Pond's Creek and Pearce Creek, fronted by the very upper head of the east side of Chesapeake Bay, and was always referred to as the Beach Farm. A man from New Jersey finally acquired this farm, had it surveyed, and laid it off into building lots. They began to sell, and so the first development of another residential area was under way. West View Shores consists of sixty or more homes, with many exclusive homes along the bay front. Some local folks have bought lots and built homes there, but mostly the residents are from out of state, several from New Jersey.

Another development nearby, referred to as Hazelmore, also fronts on the head of the bay and is also bound on one side by Pond's Creek. This land, which was only a large woods fifty years ago, has now been developed into a growing residential area, mostly inhabited by out of state people. It is owned and overseen by a family of people, formerly from Pennsylvania, and is a very private sort of development. Unless one lives there, he might be questioned as to why he's there.

There is a slow moving but more recent development just up inside the mouth of the Sassafras River in Grove Neck, referred to as Ches Haven. This is fronted by the Sassafras River. So far, this seems to be a mixture of summer residents and year-round residents. Recently a few houses are beginning to show, in view of the river, but back inland of the river frontage. This former farmland has, for a number of years, been owned and handled by a family of people from Philadelphia and this development also is mostly inhabited by out of state people.

Grove Point, many years ago, was a steamboat stop for the Ericson Line Bay Steamers, rerouted from Baltimore to Fredericktown up the Sassafras River. Fifty or more years ago, nearby Grove Point came to be the first public bathing beach in Sassafras Neck. At that time, a few people from Baltimore bought lots and built a few cottages. A few houses have been built in recent years, but thus far (1984) it has not been developed into anything big. About fifty years ago, a family of people from North East, MD acquired the old Reybold Wharf property along the east side of the mouth of the Elk River at the head of the bay which consisted of twenty or so acres of land. They started up a public bathing beach business, known as Crystal Beach, which prospered very well for several years with crowds of people coming from Wilmington, DE; Chester and Philadelphia, PA; and also many local people for the weekends.

The local people patronized the beach even through the weekdays in summer season. This bathing beach was rated one of the best sandy beaches in the whole upper bay area in those days. The operators eventually constructed a boardwalk all along the beach area and built a bathhouse, several concession stands, and a small dancing pavilion, all connected to the boardwalk. Back away from the beach in the grove of locust trees there were picnic tables, where people could have their picnic lunches. Even church picnics were held there quite often. The operators were good to the local people, and gave them good measure, so to speak.

A sizable tract of farmland adjoined the Crystal Beach property to the south. The owners of this land or farm were from Middletown, DE. They had this farm land surveyed, laid off in streets and building lots, and promoted the sale of the lots for the establishment of a summer cottage colony on the head of the bay known as Crystal Beach Manor; they also developed a bathing beach area with a bath house, refreshment stand, and picnic park. This venture also caught on and was soon drawing crowds of people from upper Delaware, Pennsylvania, and New Jersey, and, of course, some of the local people. Many of the out-of-staters bought lots and had cottages constructed on them. These two Crystal Beach areas flourished during the 1920s on up until the Wall Street crash of 1929.

During the later years of the Prohibition days, many of the out of state city people, such as politicians, city government peoples, and policemen were involved and caught up in rotten politics—racketeering in night clubs (speak-easy types), bootlegging, illegal whiskey business, and bribing and graft moneys. Some of this type of people found their way to Crystal Beach Manor, thus causing the rumor that this was the way the Manor got its start. Later on, some of these shady operators were caught, convicted, sentenced, and were jailed for a while.

However, after the Wall Street crash in 1929, and after the deaths of the original establishers and operators, followed by World War II and changes of ownership over the years, the beaches are now slowly turning into overcrowded trailer parks, and are in general run down conditions. What was once prosperous farm land, a thriving public wharf and bay, and river commerce business is now a trashy looking area overrun with mostly out-of-state, city type people—who are, like everyone else, some good, some not so good. These areas have very poor sewage disposal and roads and streets in need of repair.

Just to the north of Crystal Beach, along the mouth of Elk River and Cabin John Creek lays a tract of land which used to be referred to as the Arnold's Bar Farm. A beautiful area when it was tilled by local farmers, it has fallen prey in very recent years to an operator who has turned the waterfront area into an overcrowded trailer (RV) park known as Buttonwood Beach.

All the foregoing mentioned areas that have been developed and are still being developed, have enticed many out of state people into the confines of Sassafras Neck, and especially the west end areas of the neck that border the rivers and the head of the bay. Most of these out-of-staters come from Pennsylvania, New Jersey, and some from New York metropolitan areas, and they are much different in their ways of life and living styles, and more aggressive than the local country people.

The country folks, even the younger generations of today, are an easier going type of people, and this difference has caused a little friction in schools, churches, local fire companies, auxiliaries, and other organizations. Country people are slower to change, whereas city type people and big town folks are forever changing this, that, or the other. For instance, country folks, even in these modern times, do not try to live, or want to live the same as city people, whereas it seems that city folks like it in the country, but want to bring their city way of life with them, so to speak, and run everything in the country areas the way they would like, many times disregarding the natives in order to have their way.

It has always seemed to me that city people and country people have somewhat the same relation to one another as cats and dogs. They will sometimes tolerate each other, but will not completely mix. However, with all the undesirable "pushy" types of newcomers, there have been some families of people that have migrated to Sassafras Neck areas that are not the loud "pushy" types and are nice people that fit in well with the local folks. The Sassafras Neck local native folks would gladly welcome some of the less loud and pushy types of newcomers.

V.W. Taylor built home in Cecilton

CHAPTER XIX
MARINAS AND BOAT ACTION

In the mid-1930s, a small yacht type boat yard was established along the west end of the Sassafras River Bridge (Route 213) at Fredericktown. This operator/proprietor installed a small railway on which he would haul out small boats and yachts and do repair work and painting work on them and store some of them on the small area of land adjacent to the river for the winter.

I would suppose this operator did handle a couple dozen craft during his first year. However, each succeeding year his business greatly increased. Whether he realized it or not, he had gotten into the business at the right time, as this was to be the start of a great big marina business in the Sassafras River at the Georgetown/Fredericktown area, which would later attract other marina operators from out of the native Sassafras Neck area.

Despite the competition, this little marina at Fredericktown did continue to thrive and grow and in a few years, was quite a sizable marina. The original proprietor, after some length of time, decided to sell out and did, to a local Kent County man and son who resided just over the bridge in the village of Georgetown. These people expanded the business even more by acquiring more shoreline property just down river from the west end of the bridge. By this time, many dozens of yachts, small, medium, and large, were filling the east side of the river at Fredericktown nearly to capacity. It now was not a small marina business, but a big marina business.

The older man of this second ownership was getting old and in poor health and died leaving his son in charge of the business. By this time, pilings had been driven and many pier areas had been constructed outward into the river and were roofed over for slips where large yachts could be berthed and placed under cover for the winter months. Even quite a large retail store had been in operation, selling groceries and boat and marina supplies to the boat people. This second owner/operator in the early 1970s also sold out to another party (non-resident).

Thus, the third owner is the current proprietor as of this writing. This third owner has expanded even more and in the summer of 1979, two hundred boats, more or less, were docked at this marina, which is now going by the name of the Sassafras Boat Company. This third owner even expanded the marina to the east side of the river, having acquired the old Woodall Lumber and Farm Supply Company of Baltimore, and it is now part of the Sassafras Boat Company and berths approximately seventy-five to one hundred boats. However, this is not the only marina in the Georgetown/Fredericktown area of the Sassafras River region, which has become a substantial harbor for yachts, large and small.

Other people acquired waterfront properties in this same general area, and at the present time (1984) there are six marinas stuffed in this area at the head of the river, all clamoring to get more permits to drive more pilings and to build more slips, to entice more boats up the river, which is now so over crowded with pleasure boats that the river channel is only a narrow slot between rows and rows of tied up boats. Yet, somehow federal permits have been granted to allow more and more crowding in of boats, slips and piers.

During the good weather months of the year, May through December, the small boats, cruisers, large yachts, and sailboats, practically all owned by nonlocals and out- of-staters, are very active up and down the Sassafras River on out into the head of the bay.

The Sassafras River is a picturesque river with many creeks and coves along both sides of the river. Almost any weekend during the summer months, this river swarms with boats and yachts buzzing back and forth, across, up and down the river and the coves and creeks are filled with boats at anchor during the weekends.

The local people who own boats seldom venture out on the Sassafras or the Bohemia Rivers in the summer season, on weekends especially, for fear of getting run down and sunk by so many ill-mannered and disrespectful so-called yachtsmen, who seem to almost totally disregard many marine laws regarding overall safety of other boating people, apparently thinking that the rivers belong exclusively to them.

Many of these types of boat operators drive and operate automobiles on the highways in exactly the same manner, endangering and many times causing accidents that cripple and kill people. My son owns a boat, and we used to enjoy an occasional ride down the Sassafras to Betterton and the head of bay rivers, and also liked to take some of his friends for water skiing, but due to the hordes of reckless boaters, had to give it up, as we were getting nearly run down several times.

These great fleets of marina boats in the Sassafras River and other nearby rivers, have caused considerable pollution, especially in the Sassafras River in the way of human excrement and other human wastes, to the point that any local person would think twice before going bathing or water skiing in the river on account of the pollution therein. The Sassafras used to be a good river for fishing and crabbing, until all the marinas and boat people crowded in. A few of the local people (fisherman) used to make part of their living out of this river, but not anymore, as most of the fish have been scared and polluted out of the river.

Along the northern side of the Sassafras Neck peninsula runs the Bohemia River, with its mouth emptying into the Elk River, which in turn empties in to the head of the Chesapeake Bay. The Bohemia River is also getting cluttered with marinas and boats and people. Along the Sassafras Neck side of the Bohemia River there are three marinas, plus a small one in Scotsman Creek. There are two marinas on the northern side of the Bohemia near its mouth. So, one can see that the west end of Sassafras Neck is, in season, pretty well hemmed in with boats and boat action. During the boating season of 1980 and 1981, I would venture to say that the number of boats at the marinas in the Sassafras and Bohemia Rivers of Sassafras Neck would number in the neighborhood of six to seven hundred, and although they come in many sizes, are all pleasure boats and yachts.

As of the winter of 1980, the gasoline and fuel situation had again become a little tight and prices were rising considerably over a dollar a gallon for gas. The government was pleading with people to conserve as much as they could on fuels and energies, but got very little response. In fact, the more the pleadings increased to conserve energies and fuels, the more pleasure-bent many people got. As in the case of the Sassafras Neck area, with pleasure boats numbering near seven hundred, many of which had large-size, high horse power, gas-consuming motors churning up and down the waterways every weekend, one could easily imagine the excessive amount of gasoline burned up on a weekend, or even during the weekdays. Also, consider that most of these pleasure crafts belonged to out of state people who required travelling roundtrip from their out of state homes to the various Sassafras Neck marinas involving distances of one hundred to as much as two hundred fifty miles.

So, with a little bit of math one will find that the pleasure boat action in the Sassafras Neck area on a pleasure boating weekend could mean that approximately twenty thousand gallons of gasoline or other types of fuels were used here—and Sassafras Neck is just one small area in the vicinity of the Chesapeake Bay.

The Chesapeake Bay reported over three hundred thousand boat registrations not long ago, and this does not include all the out of state boats that come into the bay. The Chesapeake Bay is a small area. If one thinks in terms of the East Coast, and then the whole nation, those quantities become astronomical. Many years ago, out of state people from the big towns and cities used to take a vacation (two weeks) during the summer, and unless they owned a cottage somewhere, they usually returned back to the city; but the way things are now, people vacation almost every weekend, all year round. One can only guess as to how long these pleasure bent, fuel consuming folks will be able to continue on their pleasure sprees.

Sassafras River Marina in the 1980s

VINCENT TAYLOR

CHAPTER XX
BYGONE AND PRESENT TIMES

We have read in the preceding chapters of the earlier days in Sassafras Neck and of its people—their lives and activities, their ways and their customs, their times and troubles and even of their children and grandchildren, from back in the early 1900s into the 1980s.

Much of this chapter is actually somewhat of a summary of the foregoing chapters. As you have probably often heard it said by people my age (I am in my seventies as I write this) it seems that older people and younger people of today have lived in two very different worlds in regards to our lifestyles. The first thirty to thirty-five years of my life was not too much different from the horse and buggy days of my parents and grandparents.

Then, after World War II, the changes started coming fast, due to technology, higher education, scientific breakthroughs and many varied and faster means of travel such as automobiles, speed boats, private planes, jet planes, space ships and much, much more. Also, radio and television changed everything. Agricultural work started being done by mammoth tractors and equipment for the tilling and harvesting of crops, operated hydraulically and with push button control. The list goes on.

Let us now go back, say seventy or eighty years ago. The Sassafras Neck area was a quiet and beautiful area of land, dotted with farms, a few quaint little towns and crossroads villages here and there, with their country stores, shops, and country churches, country roads, and country people, who for the most part, all knew one another and in many cases related to one another.

In these bygone years, the rivers, creeks, marshes, and woodlands were clean with ample fish, game and wildlife for all. The rivers and the bay carried on much commerce by tugboat and barges, sailing schooners, small freight boats and steamboats. The railroads were much in use. Back in those days, most any sort of work or any activity by one individual, a group, or even by companies, was always carried out in a quiet, orderly, and easy going fashion for the most part.

Sassafras Neck people, due to their basic types of work—farming, fishing, carpentry, and shop keeping—worked hard and long days and were many times tired, but seldom complained of it. Even back in those days, everyone took time off for Sunday in respect for the Sabbath. Most of the time, farmers, carpenters, and shop workers did not work on Saturday afternoons, unless for emergencies or at wheat harvest.

In the old days the Sassafras Neck people lived close to God, the land, the rivers, the bay, and old Mother Nature. One used to rise up in the morning in the spring of the year and could smell the odor of fish (herring and shad) moving up into the head of the bay and into the fresh water rivers and creeks to spawn. Then, in late spring and early summer, the odor of wild flowers, honeysuckle hedgerows, and the smell of sweet clover hay permeated the land. In summertime, there was the scents of ripening wheat, cantaloupe, and watermelon. In late summer and early fall the earth smelled of green corn starting to ripen and fields freshly plowed for the sowing of winter wheat. In the frosty fall of the year and winter mornings and evenings, you could smell wood smoke wafting across the countryside, coming from homes that in the old days were heated by wood burning stoves and fireplaces.

During the night in the wintertime on moonlit nights, one could lay awake in bed and listen to various neighboring dogs barking in the distance, the occasional yap of a prowling fox and the hooting owls, then early in the mornings, to the crowing of the roosters in the poultry yards all around. There were many other night sounds depending on the season such as wild ducks quacking in the creeks and marshes, the drumming of bullfrogs, the tinkling of tink-tanks in creeks and ponds, and the sound of the horses and cattle grazing in the meadows and fields.

In the river and creek areas of Sassafras Neck, many ospreys and bald eagles used to come nest in time for the spring runs of fish which would come up the bay to feed and spawn.

Back in those days, there were no crowds of incoming people, no hordes of pleasure seekers with their speed boats, autos and motorcycles speeding up and down the roads and rivers, or planes filling the air, obliterating not only the old country day and night sounds, but much of the wildlife making those sounds.

Sassafras Neck changed over the years as any area is bound to do, but maybe a little more slowly and as needed, and not just for the sake of change itself, or to appease some individual, minority group, or clique simply because he or they were bored. Sassafras Neck got a bad blow from the Great Depression of 1929 and the 1930s, from which it never did recover. Many people gave up farming and tilling of the soil, as they just could not make it, and sold out and moved away or tried to do something else to make a living. Younger people saw the struggles and downfalls of their elders and looked elsewhere for work in the cities and larger towns. In the 1930s, strangers from up country and the cities who had money bought up quite a lot of the neck area farmland for next to nothing.

As time went on in the 1930s, the nation began to recover from the depression. Then World War II was getting under way. Factories began to hum with all kinds of work for the war effort. The prices and wages went up. Shipyards were getting busy and people were making money, except servicemen who were getting involved in the war. As people were making money, they were buying new things such as automobiles, sporting goods and radios, and were beginning to go on weekend pleasure trips to beaches along the coast, the Delmarva Peninsula, Chesapeake and Delaware Bays, and began to swarm into Sassafras Neck to seek pleasure and partake of its bay front, rivers, and creeks.

As people move about and shift around, the city slicker types of realtors, promoters and developers move right along with them to be in on the "kill," so to speak—the promoters promote areas for housing sites, the developers move in on choice sites to build homes, apartments, and shopping centers, and the realtors then sell it all.

As of these writings, (1981-1984), the old days typical of Sassafras Neck are gone and so are many of the native people. Many people now populate the necks that come in mostly from out of state such as Delaware, Pennsylvania, New Jersey, New York and, of course, some from even further away. Many of the newcomers are retired people living in some of the recently developed areas near the waterfronts.

In the years following World War II, these nice areas were "discovered," as the saying goes, and when this happens the crowds move in fast and in numbers that the native people cannot cope with, and in this present day and age (1985), it is going on all up and down the Delmarva Peninsula, and indeed in many areas all across the nation. For instance, the whole state of Florida is practically inundated with out-of-state people, and the native Floridians are much in a minority and are really getting pushed around by these hordes of newcomers.

As of this writing gasoline is $1.25 to $1.30 a gallon and fuel oil and diesel around $1.20 a gallon. New automobiles, range in price from $6,000 to $15,000 depending on size and make and many people are on buying sprees, even though many or most are heavily in debt—yet the sprees continue. How? It is hard to answer and is anybody's guess just how long the rampage will continue.

So, we natives of the old Sassafras Neck, knowing that we will soon be outnumbered, just carry on as best we can and wonder just how everything will finally wind up. We now sometimes say amongst ourselves that we sort of feel in a little way like the Native Indians who were overcome and overrun by hordes of white men from across the ocean.

At the present time, the whole of the Chesapeake Bay area is under a great strain put upon it by accelerated manufacturing and power plants and their chemical waste and run-off, over-plowed chemically fertilized farmland topsoil, thousands upon thousands of pleasure boats running up and down the bay and its tributaries with much of their wastes going overboard into the bay, sewer plant spillages into the bay and tributaries, and many other types of pollution. As the bay is, so are the waters of Sassafras Neck.

As a native "Sassafras Necker," I have truly lived in two different kinds of worlds—one in the older bygone days that was a quiet, home-style, beautiful place in which I was raised and lived—and another in recent years, that was in a land of many changes in occupation, transportation, schooling, religion, landscape and lifestyle.

I have written this little book about Sassafras Neck, so that my children, grandchildren and old native friends could read about and recall how nice a place Sassafras Neck used to be when one could, by merely asking permission from any property owner or tenant, walk or hunt in any woods, get to any river or creek to put a boat overboard, or just take a walk, or go swimming and fishing.

Now-a-days, much of the Sassafras Neck farmland is in the hands of outlanders and speculators who only seem to know how to plow up thousands of acres of land, saturate it with chemical fertilizers, and plant mostly corn. The necks are populated with many out-of-staters, mostly city folk; many pleasure seekers come and go with their campers, boats and motorcycles, congregating in in crowded camps and filling the rivers with boats, noise, and confusion, driving fish and wildlife out of the rivers and woods. One used to see swarms of bees. Now even the bees have disappeared from Sassafras Neck.

So it goes now in Sassafras Neck, and so it is with many other nice areas across the land; we old "Sassafras Necker's" are not alone in the trials and tribulations of changing scenes and disappearing traditions of the olden times.

Betterton Beach in the 1980s

ABOUT THE AUTHOR

Vincent Walmsley "Vince" Taylor was born June 5, 1912 in Earleville, (Cecil County) Maryland, the son of James Veasey and Eva Virginia Taylor. Vince grew up in and around his father's and uncle's blacksmith and wagon shop and his grandfather's farm nearby.

He was always an outdoor person all of his life and loved hiking, trapping and wild duck and rabbit hunting in the woods and marshes. As a teenager he worked on several farms and in the blacksmith shop and after graduating from the local high school, was hired in the 1930s as a boatman by the U.S. Engineer Department Baltimore to work on hydro-graphic surveys in the Chesapeake Bay Area. He was later hired as a welder in the Posey & Jones shipyard in Wilmington, Delaware where they built liberty ships for World War II.

In the 1940s, Vince was drafted into the U.S. Navy where he wound up a quarter master in piloting and navigation, and went overseas during World War II to work on a destroyer escort ship for convoy duty to New Guinea, the Philippines, Okinawa Japan. After the war he was hired by a New York engineering company for construction work on bridges, tunnels, turnpikes and dams along the Mid-Atlantic coastal area from Connecticut to Cape Fear, North Carolina.

After 28 years he retired from the engineering company and worked another 12 years doing carpenter work and painting for local people out of his home in Sassafras Neck. He also carved many old style decoys, miniature geese and marsh birds and made small Chesapeake Bay model boats. Vince also loved music, especially the accordion, on which he played various hymns and ballads to which his wife, Susie, would sing along.

Vince and Susie married in 1935 and had three children, four granddaughters, seven great-grandsons and twin great-granddaughters. Vince was a member of Old Zion Methodist Church in Cecilton, the National Rifle Association and the Baltimore Engineering Society.

He hoped to be remembered by his friends and neighbors as a "plain old outdoor country boy."

HISTORIC AND NOTEWORTHY LOCATIONS

ANCHORAGE   One and a half mile N. of Cecilton on Rt. 213. Built by the Lusby family. Home of Commodore Jacob Jones.

ARNOLD'S BAR   South West mouth of Cabin John's Creek on Elk River in Pearce's Neck.

BEAUFORTS FARM   AKA FORD's LANDING   Located in the West end of Veazey's Neck on the Elk River. Named for Ford Family. Steamboat stopping port between Baltimore & Philadelphia.

BOHEMIA ACADEMY   St. Francis Xavier Church AKA Old Bohemia Church near Warwick Md.

CABIN JOHN's CREEK   A small bay between Pearce's Neck & Veazey's Neck on Elk River.

CASH'S CORNER   One mile E. of Cecilton on Rt. 282 at junction of Ward's Hill Rd.

CASSIDY'S WHARF   Peach Blossom Farm waterfront on Sassafras River. Historic peach orchard & wharf.

CECILTON   AKA   CECIL CROSSROADS, SAVINGTON , & MORGAN'S CROSSROADS.

CHERRY GROVE   In Veazey's Neck. The ancestral home of Gov. Thomas Ward Veazey.

ESSEX LODGE   Brick farmhouse located one mile from St. Stephen's Episcopal Church on Glebe Rd. near Earleville. Veazey family home for many years.

FINGERBOARD SCHOOL   Located W. of Scotchman's Creek one mile N. of St. Stephen's Church.

FREDERICKTOWN   Located on banks of Sassafras River AKA Pennington Point or Happy Harbor.

FRISBY'S DELIGHT   AKA Rich Neck farm & England family. Four miles SW of Earleville on Sassafras River.

GINN'S CORNER   Junction on Warwick to Sassafras Rd. @ Ward's Hill Rd.

GREENFIELD'S   Farm with Brick home on SE. side of Cecilton on Rt. 213. Home of Colonel John Ward.

GRINDSTONE CORNER   Junction of Grove Neck & Pond's Neck Rds. Old site of Taylor's Blacksmith shop.

GROVE NECK   Shoreline property @ junction of Sassafras & Elk River's in Grove Neck.

HACK'S POINT   Small resort village on S. banks of Bohemia River. Named for the Hack family.

JOHNTOWN   Small village on Rt. 282 (Crystal Beach Rd.) between Earleville & Crystal Beach. Home of St. Paul's Methodist Church.

KNIGHT'S ISLAND   An Island like point on the Sassafras River off Sandy Bottom Rd, home of John Knight.

MEGILL'S CORNER   Only thru road R hand turn @ Pinewood Rd. off Rt.282 between Johntown & Reybold's Wharf (Crystal Beach).

ORDINARY POINT   Point of land running out into Sassafras River from Cecil Co. shoreline.

PEACH BLOSSOM FARM   Six miles W. of Cecilton on Sassafras

River. Historic peach orchard, Cassidy's Wharf.

PEDDLER'S LANE   Old name for Earleville. Peddler's Lane is still a street in Earleville.

QUINN HOUSE   Brick home in Warwick built by Daniel Charles Heath. Known as a stopping point for George Washington on Rt. 282.

REED'S CORNER   Junction of Rt.282 & Sandy Bottom Rd. near Earleville.

RICH HILL   Plantation on head of Sassafras River owned by St. Augustine Church from Alexander Baird.

ROSE HILL   Marsh family Plantation on Sassafras River four miles S. of Earleville. Inherited by Gen. Thomas Foreman inherited from his grandfather Thomas Marsh.

STRAWBERRY HILL   Located between Little Bohemia Creek & Worsell Manor AKA Vulcans Roost.

WARWICK   Founded by the Heath family. On Rt. 282 E. of Cecilton near Del. St. Line.

WATTS CORNER   Intersection of Pond Neck & Stemmers Run Rds. Two miles W. of Earleville.

WHITEHALL   Old Eldridge family farm on E. side of Rt. 213 approx. one mile N. of Fredericktown.

WOODLAWN   On Grove Point Rd. three miles SW. of Earleville on Sassafras River. Home of Thomas Ward one of the founders of St. Stephens Episcopal Church in Earleville.

WORSELL MANOR   Home of the Heath family three miles E. of Cecilton. Gen. George Washington dined and lodged there on his travels. Original owner was Peter Sayer.

References: Familysearch.org (Earleville, Cecil County, Maryland, Genealogy); Wikipedia.org; National Register of Historic Places; Earnest A. Howard Genealogy & History Fact File; Cecil County Historical Society; Maryland Manual online; and Maryland State Archives Website.

Note: Some locations may or may not appear on local, county or state recognized maps.

Vincent W. Taylor and his family

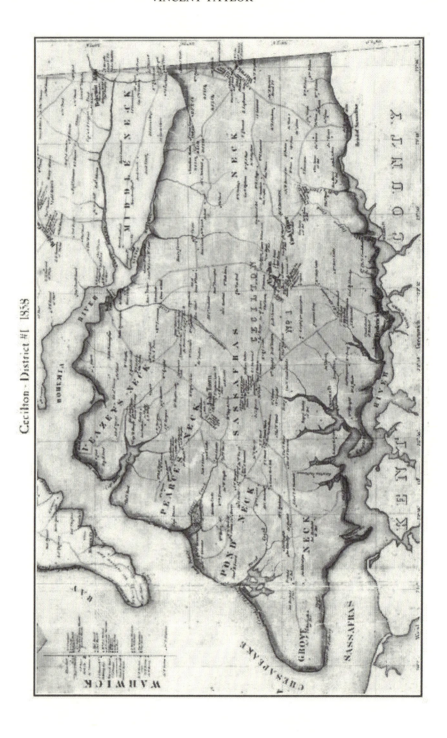

Dear Pop...We finally got it done!

- The Kids

Made in the USA
Middletown, DE
25 May 2021